SACRED & OVERFLOWING

SACRED & OVERFLOWING

A 30 Day Devotion to the Woman God Called You to Be

KONYKA DUNSON

Carnelian Moon Publishing

Published by Carnelian Moon Publishing

www.carnelianmoonpublishing.com

Cover Design by Jennifer Insignares
Cover Photo by Sachin C Nair
Interior Layout Design by Simon Brimble

Printed Book ISBN: 978-1-7375582-3-1
eBook ISBN: 978-1-7375582-5-5

For the women who lifted me

My Grandmothers

Alyce K. Barnett and Lucy B.W. Dunson

My Mother

Brenda E.B. Dunson

Acknowledgments

To say this book has been a journey is an understatement. It unfolded over several years with the loving support of many. My mother, Brenda Dunson, and my grandmothers, now my heavenly angels, Alyce Barnett and Lucy Dunson, are the women who lifted me. To them, I owe the deepest, most abiding gratitude. They encouraged my voice, loved me, laughed with me, and always listened. And for my mom, who always and endlessly believed, I am forever grateful. To my family, my dad, Edward Dunson, and my brother, Kenan Dunson, who all support me no matter what—I truly thank you.

While working on this book, I spent many days at diners, writing for hours and drinking lots of coffee! I am grateful to the waiters, some who became blessed friends along the way, who encouraged me and always filled my cup. To dear friends, I have known for decades, who have supported me at many steps of my journey, and Lenora and Nakia, who heard my ideas over brunches and dinners, I thank you!

To the people who helped shape the book into reality, I am grateful. To the church communities of Silver Spring Church of Christ and Zion Church Landover, I am forever grateful for the community, to connect, love, and grow in Christ together. Thank you to Kristin Clark for the editorial direction, consultation, and editing to lay a solid foundation for the project. Thank you to Cathy McMahen, for the final proofreading to bring this project to a beautiful close. To my first readers of the manuscript, Sherre, Shawn, Angelina, Zarena, and Chrisa, thank you for the positive words that gave me a boost on the project while this book was still in becoming. To Aliya, thank you for all the "input" and for helping me see the uniqueness of this path. And Tramaine, who always encouraged me to share my voice and write over the years, I thank you! To Keith Lee, who challenged me, loved me, exhorted me to share my voice, and pressed me to write, and importantly, to finish, thank you. I am grateful for every push and our cherished conversations, a wonderful part of this journey.

To Debbie and Judy of Carnelian Moon Publishing, your overwhelming, all-encompassing positive energy was a blessing. To work with you, as you sowed your own belief into me, was the absolute best way to launch this book into the world. To the many inspirational women, some I know from afar, some up close, and some who show up on the pages in the book, I thank you. The shining light of your example inspired me to shine my light, in my own way, and bring forth this book.

I am immensely grateful for all the love, inspiration, and support, from so many, in so many ways, that helped make this book a reality. With all my heart and soul, and sacred and overflowing gratitude, I truly thank you.

Contents

Introduction

I have always known there was a God. An omniscient, sovereign, Holy Presence who freely gives love, help, and guidance. As a little girl in Sunday school, I sang it out loud, "Yes, Jesus Loves Me!" I knew God loved me, and you couldn't tell me otherwise. Yet, through the years, in that passage from girl to woman, there were moments where I hit a bump in the road. A deep and serious one, like a crater. And I really, really, really...needed God. I had so many questions and needed direction. Although I continually prayed, I still felt like my life purpose was off-center, muddy, and unclear. I simply needed God to show me the way forward.

After a setback in graduate school, where I decided to leave the program, I was at a major impasse. I didn't know what would unfold and where my life was taking me. I was in that quintessential search for meaning and mission. I prayed a lot for clarity, direction, and my next steps. I asked, somewhat jokingly, for an indisputable sign. I wished I would wake up in the middle of the night to find Jesus sitting at the foot of my bed in all His glory, with a bright and burning light illuminating the darkness. Then, he would proclaim, "Behold, Konyka ... this is your purpose." At once, the search, mystery, wondering, and all the questions would be all over. The confusion would instantly vanish, and with absolute certainty, I would proceed—knowing exactly what I was meant to do. Well, as much as I prayed and prayed and even sang "Jesus loves me," that never happened.

Instead, God gave me the blessed opportunity to live my life, embrace my own experiences, and dig deep into my soul. God gave me the space to figure it out, to live it out, and to lean deeply into prayer. I brought every challenge, every tear, every question, and every idea to God. I found a sacred place of communing with God. Slowly and over time, I found the next steps on the path, light along the way, and the clarity I was seeking. And I found this essential truth: your soul with God is the blueprint. In your own sacred relationship with God, you find the wisdom, guidance, and direction to enlighten your journey step by blessed step.

Our lives are the fertile ground, where all that God has endowed in our souls springs forth and beautifully grows. Yet, precisely, because we do not get a clear manual, sometimes the path is dark and vague. On our divine paths, we learn to explore the depths of our own life lessons, trust, and listen to the stirring in our souls. I learned to draw strength from my faith. I learned to value all that moves in my being and soul as a woman—regardless of whether it is different, unknown, too bold, or understood by others. I learned to trust the sacred path I walk with God.

In a multitude of ways, our paths are unique, as they are the new territory of our lives. Yet, it is all the sacred province of God. There, we find the cherished part of us that dwells most closely with God. And I have found, as I called on God for help to make sense of life in crucial moments, I received insight and revelation. Yet, I also felt this beautiful inner space, inviting me to connect with a revelation within. As I had once prayed for Jesus to appear with utter and profound clarity, I felt God calling me to answer the question from my own soul: Who have I called you to be?

In all my searching, seeking, and praying, I found a deeper appreciation of all that God endowed in my soul and life. I began to trust, honor, and live what God has placed within and before me. In our own paths, we awaken to the sacred significance of our own journey, a deeper understanding of ourselves, and our own connection with God. That path is varied, from woman to woman, but it is yours. In your own sacred relationship with God, you tap into the overflow—your center of purpose overflowing with blessings, gifts, and grace that flows freely to you and from you. There, you find the unmistakable beauty and power of the woman God called you to be.

This book, in many ways, is what I needed and always wanted to read on that soulful path. A book that spoke to the journey I was on with God, that honored my path and the lives of women around me. Our souls are precious, ordained by God with a mighty, divine, and powerful calling. Yet, our life calling does not have a fully detailed blueprint—at least not one fully visible to us. While you may have guides, friends, and counselors along the way, no one can chart the path for you. Some people may be profoundly helpful, while others can be distractors or detractors. I arrived at this essential truth—I needed to sit with God, express all that was in my soul, and listen. In this sacred communion, you enter a profound relationship with a loving God, who guides your path, and lights the way as you embrace, honor, and step into your calling.

This book is a "devotion," which means to honor, love, and become dedicated to what is sacred. This book "devotion" is to you—to the woman God called you to be. The purpose is simple: On your own soulful journey, allow space to honor all that is divine, all that is within you, your life experiences, and the beauty of your soul. It is an invitation: Sit with God, with your heart wide open, and behold with gratitude all that God has endowed in your soul. It is an offering: Reflect deeply, appreciate your own wisdom, challenges, joys, and triumphs. It is a calling: Let your own voice rise and lift your soul and your prayers to God.

Over the span of thirty days, this devotion takes you on a journey. We begin with your deepest identity: who you are with God, at the depths of your soul and mind, and your own covenant with God. Next, we explore connecting personally with God: forging your own sacred relationship and being attuned with God and your own highest purpose. We navigate trust, knowing God on your path, and honoring your calling. Finally, we honor the gifts of your soul—the glorious energy of your love, voice, and vision that carries a divine purpose.

This book is filled with insights and lessons learned from a deeply personal place within me. Each day begins with Scripture and then draws upon a wealth of women's wisdom: insights from lived experience, stories of women in the Bible, authors, poets, historical figures, and personal moments of meaning. I share my experiences of how I more deeply connected with God, and at many junctures, found His blessed light. I explore my fears, doubts, roadblocks, and, importantly, how they fell away. Finally, I explore the blessed challenges, breakthroughs, and triumphs that brought my soul close to God.

Ultimately, in the spirit of devotion to you, I offer each day to spark, inspire, and catalyze your own reflection, contemplations, and prayers. At the end of each day, there is a devotion, a sacred prayer. Then, I invite you to write your own devotion. There are questions and space for you to reflect, meditate, and pour out your own answers. My prayer is that as you embark on this journey, you find a more profound gratitude for the woman God called you to be. I pray that you enter into greater dimensions of your relationship with God and cultivate a deeper sense of your own soulful wisdom.

Over the years, I have found women often struggle with their greatest challenges privately, behind closed doors, and often alone. Baring our souls, going deep with God, and surrendering everything lightens our loads and invites in what our souls need most. As much as I needed to find wisdom in my own relationship with God, I genuinely needed to connect with other women. Our journeys are our own, yet amazingly universal. We are all on a soulful path. We can bring light and blessings to each other.

Finally, this book is a soulful conversation, connecting the wisdom of God, your soul, and many, many women. I pray that what stirs in your soul grows stronger, louder, and brighter. I hope you engage an even deeper realization and profound gratitude of the blessing that lies in your soul, purpose, life, and calling.

This book may very well become a blessed companion, a gift returned back to you. By the time you have read and worked through each day, your own insights, reflections, and prayers will be written. Your words may become an offering to give to a daughter, share with a mother, discuss with a grandmother, sister, colleague, or neighbor. Your words may become the light in the darkness that illuminates another woman's path. Perhaps you will gather in a sacred circle with friends and share what you have never shared before. Ultimately, this devotion becomes your wisdom, your light, a piece of your journey with God.

Your calling is sacred and powerful, a divine summoning to the woman God created you to be. That calling must be shared. Our individual and collective missions bring to light where we stand. We have many junctures and opportunities to use our God-given talents, all that moves our soul, to love, create, change, build, inspire, and heal. As God blesses, we are also blessings, radiating immense light much-needed in our lives, families, communities, and throughout our world.

With my heart open and my soul full, my prayer is that this devotion is a blessing to you. I pray that you experience a deeper, more profound gratitude for your journey, experiences, wisdom, your walk with God, and for the woman God has called you to be. I pray that you enter into a deep communion with God, free of all barriers or limitations, and feel God's overflowing love. I pray that you honor and appreciate every step of your journey, the missteps, as well as the good and solid ones. I pray that new possibilities stir within your soul to share your gifts and that God's blessings flow freely to you and through you. On your journey and in these next 30 days, I pray that you find, deep in your soul, all that is sacred and overflowing.

THEME ONE

Your Soul-Deep Identity

Identity is the fundamental way we know ourselves. It can be constructed of many factors and multiple layers, including our ethnicity, culture, religion, career, or nationality. Yet, your soul-deep identity, given by God, is constructed within your mind, heart, and soul. It is an identity that goes deep within and transcends any external factors. This identity defines the essence of who you are – your way of being, of feeling, of knowing who you are, uniquely and divinely. This identity resides in your soul.

The expression of your soul is sacred. It is the essence God has endowed deep within you, at your central core. It is your divine fingerprint. There will never be another you. Embracing, cultivating, and honoring your soul-deep identity is the foundation of the woman God called you to be.

The first three days of this book focus on your soul-deep identity. We begin with defining identity through the lens of God as women who are wonderfully and purposefully created. Next, we explore the centrality of the love of God in our identities. Finally, we delve into drawing strength from your soul-deep identity—the power of knowing, in all of life, who God created and called you to be.

Day 1

To Embrace the Woman God Created You to Be

I will give thanks to You, for I am fearfully and wonderfully made; Wonderful are Your works, And my soul knows it very well.

Psalms 139:14 NASB1995

Our mothers have a sacred responsibility. To be themselves, the woman God calls them to be, and all the while: nurturing, guiding, and ushering their daughters into the women God created them to be. My own mother, with her unflinching resolve and unending care, created so many precious memories. For my birthdays, she joyfully hosted epic three-day slumber parties, squeezing six little girls into her Volkswagen Bug from Friday night to Sunday morning for a weekend of fun. And as I think back, perhaps she enjoyed it as much as we did!

Mom would often share a memory that planted a vision that stayed with me. Holding her newborn daughter, she looked at me and saw a twinkling look in my eyes, as though I could not wait to get started living life. She said, "*She's* going to be a star." Her words never felt like a dramatic declaration or a role she expected me to fulfill. Rather, a genuine observation, a deep sense of knowing about her own daughter—she saw the spark of light in her daughter's soul, what is precious and divine.

This light in the soul, the spark within us from God, holds the nature of who we fundamentally are. As we grow, year to year, from one life stage to the next, the spark of the soul enlivens and expands as we experience what we are drawn to and resonate with. In elementary school, I loved listening to stories of courageous heroes in Black History Month, especially the women. I was utterly fascinated with Harriet Tubman – a woman so determined to deliver her people to freedom that she carried a gun to deter anyone who would even *think* of going backward. I wondered how she could possess such courage and boldness in the face of such danger. As a little girl, her spirit inspired me.

Ever since then, and to this very day, I admire trailblazing, phenomenal women who follow the call of their own soul, like Maya Angelou. The extraordinary poet, author, teacher, and woman of profound wisdom—seemed to possess a knowledge of her identity deep in her spirit and moved with power and certainty. I am fascinated, not because they are famous, but because they are bold. They are bright lights, rising to and realizing their grandest God-given potential. I wanted to feel that within myself.

I, too, wanted to realize a deep sense of identity, connect to a deeper purpose, and feel intrinsic power grounded in my very essence and reason for being. While I enjoyed successes, academic and creative accomplishments, I still felt something was missing. During challenging times, I felt a nagging sense of uncertainty, not being totally secure in the path I was walking.

Yet, while I felt a pull within me toward some grand purpose, I didn't quite know how to live it, be it, or even get there. Like the women I admired, I wanted an indomitable sense of self and to know it deep down in my soul. Yet, as much as I looked longingly to them, to find my own soul-deep identity, I had to go on a very personal journey.

In the small church sanctuary, with fans slowly spinning overhead, about twenty of us sat on wooden pews studying the Psalms in Wednesday night Bible study. I was a few weeks into my first-ever Bible Study since being baptized. Every week, I attended religiously to learn and absorb the Word of God. That particular evening, I was calm, at peace, and everything felt right. Our teacher explained that the Psalms were songs of the soul, of intense longing for God laid bare and visible.

Starting at Psalms 1, we went passage by passage, meditating on the Scripture, inviting the truth to slowly unfold and seep deep within. Months later, after coming, listening, and learning, we arrive at Psalms 139. As I read the words, I felt something move deep within me. I felt a resounding, powerful energy move, as though my soul rose up and said, *Yes!*

> *13 For You formed my inward parts; You wove me in my mother's womb.*
> *14 I will give thanks to You, for I am fearfully and wonderfully made; Wonderful are Your works, And my soul knows it very well.*

My soul knows it right well. While I certainly approached Bible study, seeking wisdom, eagerly and openly, I was not expecting to find the answer my soul was seeking. Yet, that is the way of following God. A latent, background desire, deep within, nestled in my soul and kept pulling me forward...step by step. It led me through a winding path of my own spiritual seeking. It led me to be baptized as an adult woman seeking God with all my soul. It led me to a moment where I was sitting on the pew and listening—listening to who God says I am.

We are, indeed, "fearfully and wonderfully made," with reverence and awe, a marvel of God's universe, like any other natural wonderful work of God—a breathtaking vista, the endless oceans, formidable mountains, and plunging valleys. Whenever I sit in the window seat of an airplane, I savor the view below me and behold God's creation. The majestic landscape of clouds paints the horizon in endless formations of tranquility. I meditate on the unfathomable force, love, order, and beauty of all creation. It is humbling to feel the awesome blessing of knowing that the same God, who created all of this wonder, created you and me. It is almost beyond comprehension to understand God's conception of us, as fearfully and wonderfully made by God, the Creator of everything we hold in awe. Yet, that is the truth.

On that Wednesday evening, I found my soul-deep identity. I found an identity that went deeper than cultural norms, success, or even self-esteem. I found a greater depth of knowing myself as God created me. To know that I am connected to God, that I am purposefully, wonderfully, and reverently created—is the truth that holds me and inspires me.

Perceiving myself through the lens of God, I simply appreciate the wonder in my own being. The soul, the immutable, glorious part of you, holds your unique, gift-filled nature. The energetic expression of you—your heart, mind, and passion—is connected to the divine. Like energy without beginning or end, the truth within your soul is indestructible. To let the truth settle into you—that you exist because God desires you to exist—invites God's truth to exude from every pore of your being.

Knowing who you are, having the courage to be that divine being is a sacred journey. We are always with ourselves, so knowing ourselves seems like the simplest, most accessible thing we can do. Yet our consciousness, the space of knowing of self, is filled with other ideas about who we are. Identity is influenced by external factors, cultural norms around gender and ethnicity, familial and career expectations, and the circumstances in which we are born. Yet, your *soul-deep* identity, the identity that is God-given, holds your deepest truth, potential, and possibilities. That night in Bible study, I dropped my anchor and all my heart into my soul-deep identity.

The search was over. I felt the answer in my soul. I am a fearfully and wonderfully made woman created by God with a glorious purpose. The energy of your soul, all that God has uniquely endowed in you, serves a mighty God and a miraculous purpose. I began to embrace my own identity: born to share love, creativity, imagination, vision, and compassion, and serve to make a positive and powerful impact. Deep down, the essence of your soul, anchored in your connection with God, is who you truly are.

What I admired in the bold, brave women who came before me was the power in their *souls*. I understand now—this is what my mother saw when first she held me, the shining light that emanated straight from my soul. Now, I see all that is within me, and I say—*Yes, let it shine.*

The work of expressing, being, and fulfilling who we are is ongoing. As mothers embrace their children and all they can be, we embrace the woman God created us to be—the powerful identity God has ordained.

We have the sacred responsibility to define ourselves. We make the choice to birth, to live, unfold, and express the precious spark of the divine that we carry in our souls. Whether others see it, or even if you struggle to see your own soul-deep identity, God sees it. Your brilliant truth endures. To stand on the truth of who God made you to be becomes a powerful identity to build your life upon—an undeniable, ever-present, and non-changing truth.

You have the sacred and powerful decision to say Yes with your soul to all that God has endowed within you: your grandest possibilities and the powerful blessings of the woman God called you to be. It is yours, your soul-deep identity, a gift to embrace and unfold, and to let your light...shine brilliantly.

Devotion

Thank you, God, for Your eternal presence and love. Thank you for the woman You created me to be. Thank you, God, for every gift, talent, passion, and purpose You have endowed in my soul, heart, and life. Thank you for Your guidance in every step of my life as I anchor my identity with the knowledge of who You created me to be. I come before You, God, with honor and reverence. I pray for Your continued blessings as I honor, embrace and live the calling of the woman You created me to be.

Reflection

Imagine, for a moment, God's view of you with reverence and wonder. Look deeply within, into your soul. What qualities in your soul, heart, and mind (beyond the physical) do you most value, admire, and treasure?

Reflect on the qualities above and consider: How do you define your own soul-deep identity? Who has God created you to be?

Take this moment to deeply and profoundly appreciate who you are. How can you more deeply embrace and express your soul-deep identity? What has God placed in your soul to bring forward in your life calling?

Write your own devotion here.

Read it aloud and let it sink deep into your soul.

Group Discussion

Begin with each person sharing their devotion and reflections on Day 1. What does it mean to you to define your identity based on your soul? How does this differ, in any way, from other ways you may define yourself? Consider: How does viewing yourself as God views you impact how you define yourself? How does this identity expand and empower you? In closing: How can we appreciate and encourage each other as the women God has created us to be? End with prayer, lifting and supporting each woman in who God created her to be.

Day 2

Ultimate Self-Love: To Love Yourself as God Loves You

If I take the wings of the dawn, If I dwell in the remotest part of the sea, Even there Your hand will lead me, And Your right hand will lay hold of me.

Psalms 139:9-10 NASB1995

To be yourself, to be the woman God called you to be, you must *love* yourself. Somewhere in my 20s, in the throes of dating and seeking Prince Charming, I began seeing love as something that came from the outside. While I had a depth of self-esteem and positive regard for myself, love was different. To be loved so deeply, so profoundly, completely, and effortlessly was what I longed for. Sure, Hallmark movies are just movies, but the fantasy of a wonderful, genuine man, who at once lays eyes upon you and sees the beauty of your soul, inside and out, is a beautiful dream. That love is instant, magical, total, and promises to treasure you fully exactly as you are. Yet, it's a movie. The credits roll, and the actors and producers pack it up and go home. But the longing for love, unending and unconditional, stayed with me.

Fortunately, so does God. The fantasy I imagined is exactly and always God's love. Yet, the downside of longing for a fantasy—you start to believe you're missing something and chase fulfillment as though someone else supplies your answers. You miss the sacred love that you carry within. Life always brings challenges, the need for help, support, and encouragement. In our journeys of becoming and growing, love is the energy and the fuel that sustains us. It is truly sacred when we find that love and give it freely to ourselves. Like an overflowing blessing, God gives us a model for ultimate self-love: to love ourselves as God loves us.

I will never forget seeing a little girl, about six years old, riding on the bus on Capitol Hill in Washington, DC. She oozed love. Her joyous smile beamed delight, and she bounded with energy as though happiness bounced within her. As the bus lurched toward Union Station, her eyes gleamed with excitement, taking in the wonder of what seemed ordinary to everyone else—pigeons, people, and cars going by. I admired and enjoyed the love of life that beamed from her eyes.

I watched her with delight, yet her mother, seemingly, had had enough and warned her out loud, "I keep telling you you're a little girl, stop sitting like that." Then she spanked her soft soul...hard. I could feel the little girl sink into herself. She slid down into the seat, closed her legs together, and laid her little head against the window. Tears streamed down her face, and the bus rolled on. She was no longer looking out the window at the wonders of life. I felt her pain, and I turned away. I did not want to see her tears and her joyous, loving freedom turn to sad resignation.

I will never truly know how this little girl felt. She may not have even felt what I felt. It could have been a familiar moment of discipline for a mother, ensuring that her daughter would not sit in public in an "un-ladylike" manner. Yet, I know how it touched my heart. I felt her love and joy flowing so naturally within. She was so free, comfortable, and precious. As a little girl, she didn't have to search for love; she already possessed it in her spirit that loved life.

As we go through life, the journey of becoming the women we are called to be, even at a tender, young age, can be a rocky path. The love and joy so freely flowing in your soul, for many girls, becomes mixed with different ideas, unexpected limits, and binding constraints. Yet, it is still a sacred path to travel. On the path, some of us are blessed to have people who champion and love us endlessly. While some of us have gifts, desires, and visions that the people closest to us may never understand. Many of us may feel like we are walking alone. The journey to fully be yourself, to experience the fullness of your identity rooted in your soul, takes *courage*. It takes love. Love, that soulful, spiritual elixir, heals all, uplifts, and fills you with the sacred knowledge that you matter and who you are born to be matters. Blessedly, God shows us the way of universal love.

Psalms 139 reveals the love of God, the bedrock truth to strengthen your soul-deep identity: God loves you endlessly.

1 O Lord, You have searched me and known me.
2 You know when I sit down and when I rise up; You understand my thoughts from afar.
3 You scrutinize my path and my lying down, And are intimately acquainted with all my ways.

There is nothing that God does not know about us. From the moment our eyes open in the morning, as you sleep and dream at night, to every tendency you have, God knows it all.

4 Even before there is a word on my tongue, Behold, O Lord, You know it all.
5 You have enclosed me behind and before, And laid Your hand upon me

6 Such knowledge is too wonderful for me; It is too high, I cannot attain to it.

It is unfathomable to think that our moments, each and every feeling and thought, are divinely known. Every idea, every joy, struggle, and every thought about struggle, God knows it all. And His presence is inescapable.

7 Where can I go from Your Spirit? Or where can I flee from Your presence?
8 If I ascend to heaven, You are there; If I make my bed in Sheol, behold, You are there.

God is omnipresent and is with us always. To ascend to heaven is to be in the presence of God. But, to make my bed in Sheol, which is Hell, is to be unmercifully and painfully far from God. I could mess up horribly, commit the gravest sins, yet His word assures our souls—God is there. No matter what I do or what I fail to do, as I live, make mistakes, and have regrets, God is still there. No matter if Prince Charming loves me or hurts my heart, no matter the setbacks or depths of loneliness or isolation, God is there.

9 If I take the wings of the dawn, If I dwell in the remotest part of the sea.
10 Even there Your hand will lead me, And Your right hand will hold of me.

Through every obstacle, God is there—leading you and holding you. There is nothing we can do to elude God's reach and His steady, ever-present love. No matter what, God loves you. No matter how hard I might try, I cannot flee God's love. This is the greatest love of all. The love of God will never depart. Every soul is so deeply precious to God.

This kind of love may feel like fantasy, but when we know God and truly let His love settle into our souls, *that love is real.* To know that I am loved, entirely, to the core of my being, and seen and loved completely, is the deepest love imaginable. When I truly accepted and embraced the love of God, love flowed in. His love washed over and filled my heart, mind, and soul. I gave thanks to God, and I realized this truth: This is how I must love myself.

When we know love and understand it clearly and undeniably, it calls us to take action. As bell hooks' book *All About Love* beautifully reveals—we can be, create, and choose to love. To love yourself as God loves you is to see every aspect of your being and to love *all* of you. With this love, you regard, respect, and value yourself as God values you. To love yourself as God loves you, you possess a never-ending appreciation for you, your soul, no matter what, in every step of your life.

When I think of the little girl on the bus, what I know about God, whether she is affirmed, encouraged, denied, or suppressed, God will be with her. As God is with each and every one of us. God will see the shimmer of her soul when she cries and when she needs the Almighty's helping hand. Embracing the fullness of the love of God lead me to this truth: What I sought as a younger woman, I never lacked. God was holding me in an imaginable love. I had to choose to love myself as God loves me.

You have the sacred choice to love yourself and honor the woman God created you to be. To love yourself as God loves you is to let God's abundant love expand, build, and enrich your soul-deep, God-given identity. This unlimited love forges the truth of your being, as divine love fills and lifts you every step of your blessed life journey.

Devotion

Dear God, thank you for Your love that overwhelms, never leaves me, and always holds me. Your love is beyond measure. Thank you for loving me so completely and showing me how to love myself. Thank you for every moment of my journey, the deepest valleys and the highest peaks. I come before You, God, with deepest love, reverence, and gratitude. May Your love flow into my soul and fill the foundation of who I truly am. I pray for Your continued blessings as I love the woman You created me to be. Thank you, God.

Reflection

Every aspect of you is known by God. Imagine God's unending love for you. What do you love about yourself? Keep writing until you are tired!

Now, be honest: What do you not love about yourself, if anything? Reflect on what you have written. Where did this "lack of love" come from, and where are you judging yourself? Now, consider: How can you embrace and love all of you? Hold this in prayer and write down all that arises.

Consider how loving others may come very easily to you. How can you give even more love to yourself? Write specific actions.

Write your own devotion here.

Read it aloud, feel God's love and your love for yourself, and let it sink deep into your soul.

Group Discussion

Begin with each person sharing their devotion and reflections on Day 2. Name one thing that you love about each person in the group, even if you just met. What does self-love mean to you? How does the love of God expand self-love? Share your stories: How have you struggled with or found strength in self-love? How can we give more love to ourselves and the women in our lives? Close in a prayer circle, lifting each woman up to be filled with the love of God.

DAY 3

Unshakable: To Stand Strong in the Woman God Called You to be

I have set the Lord continually before me; Because He is at my right hand, I will not be shaken. Therefore my heart is glad and my glory rejoices; My flesh also will dwell securely.

Psalms 16:8-9 NASB1995

The sun was shining, and beautiful baobab trees stood in the distance. We were about an hour outside of Nairobi, Kenya, visiting a school for children, the first stop of our mission trip. Weeks before the mission trip, I began preparing. I prayed and prayed even more. I focused my intention, spirit, and heart to be fully aligned with God's will. With my soul ready to serve, I arrived open to all that would unfold.

Our mission team arrived on the school grounds prepared, in a van fully loaded with bedding, school, and personal supplies. The school, grounded in Christ, provided children a place to live, healthy meals, new friends, and an ever-so-valuable education.

One darling little girl, Joyce, with enthusiasm and a beaming smile, gave a few of us a tour of their home. She led us around the school grounds and showed me where she slept; some bare beds had no mattresses. With pride, she took us into a one-room schoolhouse building with old wooden desks. Then, she showed us their bathrooms, an outhouse with no plumbing. And finally, she took us to a thriving, vibrant garden that supplied food for the students.

We ended our tour, and I stood, gathered together in a circle with eight of her friends in the wide-open grass, with the sun shining on us. This moment with the girls, so young, elegant, and full of glee, reminded me of how I gathered with my own students in the United States. Even though I was a high school math teacher, I occasionally carved out time to gather the students in a circle. We would have a group conversation, where they could share their thoughts, feelings, and ideas. I wanted to offer insight, and importantly, to catalyze their own critical thinking.

Standing in our circle on the school grounds, I asked the girls about themselves. They were living away from their parents and shared that they do not see them often. As they spoke, I had a strong feeling pressing upon me that some of their lives would take difficult turns, the safety of the school environment would not always be there for them. I felt a compelling urge to impress upon them and share what was brimming in my soul. No matter what happens in life, they must always know—they are so very precious to God and that God is always with them.

I wanted each girl to know and let it implant deep down in her soul—the power of knowing who she is with God. Even if she felt alone, she had a God-given strength within her. No matter the difficulty that may come, whether trials with school or even her own sense of self—know who God made you to be. If anyone ever tells you that you are anything less than a fearfully and wonderfully made divine creation—remember who you are. Stand strong in knowing who God made you to be. Psalms 139:14 rose within me, words that had become my truth serum, and I poured God's truth into our sacred gathering:

"I will give thanks to You, for I am fearfully and wonderfully made; Wonderful are Your works, And my soul knows it very well."

With tears welling in my eyes, I wanted to instill as much as possible into our precious moment. I told them to grab hold of this spiritual truth, have confidence in their identity rooted in God, and know that He will be with them at every step. As I was talking, one little girl turned and walked away from the circle. For several moments, she stood on her own and seemed to be reflecting deeply. Then, slowly, she raised her head toward the sky and wiped tears from her eyes.

These little girls had challenges. While they were blessed to be in school, even that was a tenuous situation. The schools were supported by donations and the ability of parents to pay. If their families faced financial hardship, some students were not able to stay in school. Being out of school in an impoverished environment brings its own set of issues for young girls growing up. I wanted each girl to know that she has an unshakeable identity with God, rooted in their soul—where she will find her greatest strength.

I have set the Lord continually before me; Because He is at my right hand, I will not be shaken. Therefore my heart is glad and my glory rejoices; My flesh will also dwell securely.
Psalms 16:8-9 NASB1995

To know God, your powerful Protector is with you always, you stand strong. The path through life can be dimmed by many challenges. One's soulful, God-given uniqueness may not always be trumpeted and affirmed by others as a great gift. As we grow through life, we face tests of our identity. When things are going great in a career, marriage, and family, we may dwell securely in who we are and feel on top of the world. But when trials come, that security—deep down to our identities—is tested.

Professional success and prestigious positions can come and go. The greatest love relationships may soar to amazing heights, then painfully crash. Our physical appearances and body images change with time or even with a difficult disease. When we experience failure, we may question who we are. Yet, to truly dwell securely in our souls, to fundamentally know who we are, we must always dwell with God.

To know at your core that with God, you will not be shaken, despite any shifting and mounting tides around you, is a powerful, soul-deep identity. We find power in owning and claiming that truth: a soulful confidence in who you truly are. This soul-deep identity strengthens and propels you through every single turn in all of life's winding roads.

I learned to lean into this soul-deep identity. At times, I felt challenged in defining myself when things were not going well. When I found myself working in various, intermittent freelance and temporary positions, I questioned myself as not having the security of a "good" job title. I compared myself to others as I pieced together my next steps. As pressures rose, I felt like there was no steady ground, feeling blown and pushed by the turbulent winds of life. We can question who we are in those moments. I certainly did.

Yet the strong, unshakeable knowledge of God becomes the steady ground for our lives, a solid identity of who we truly are. When I came to Kenya, I was on steady ground. I knew God was with each and every one of us. I knew my identity ran deep; it was soul deep. The spirit of love, connecting with young people, flowed through my soul. That depth and expression of love, rooted in who I truly am, was part of my truest, most enduring identity.

On that day at the school grounds, the little girl who stood alone eventually returned to our circle. I knew then, God led me to speak to her. I felt blessed to see her take the time she needed, raise her face to the sun, and have her own sacred moment. I had hoped to impart a memory that would cling to her spirit, so if tough times occurred, she would remember who God made her to be. As she stood in the circle beside her friends, I smiled. Although she never shared what she was thinking, I knew both of us connected with truth in our souls. I felt assured, she would stand firm in who God created her to be.

Your knowledge of God is the solid ground to anchor your soul-deep identity. When you stand strong in who God created to be, you have a sacred life opportunity. Your gifts, your light, and your soul, filled and flowing with the love of God, become a blessing to others. You touch, love, impact, and reach others, as God has ordained. With every blessed step on the path of the woman God called you to be, your strength grows, and the blessings are sacred and overflowing.

Devotion

Heavenly Father, thank you for the blessed assurance You give that underlies every step and day of my life. Thank you, God, for Your Presence that strengthens me deep in my soul. I stand firm knowing I am with You, and You, God, are with me always. I pray for strength and Your direction, guidance, and grace. I pray that You lead me to fulfill every aspect of the woman that You created me to be. In Jesus's name, I pray and thank you, God. Amen.

Reflection

As we have spent three days on your soul-deep identity, what insights do you have about who you are at the soul level? Who did God create and call you to be?

Think deeply about God and how you connect with and know God. What strengthens you? Write practices, mantras, and all that arises.

Reflect on what matters to you now. Imagine you at your strongest and note what is true about you. In what ways can you further cultivate, strengthen, and expand your deepest identity?

Write your own devotion here.

Read it aloud, stand up and let the strength of God's love sink deep into your soul.

Group Discussion

Begin with each person sharing their devotion and reflections on Day 3. What did you discover about another that inspired or encouraged you that you did not know before? Share your stories: How have you found strength within, and what did you learn? What aspects of God's truth have you leaned on? How can we support and strengthen each other as the women God called us to be? Close in a prayer circle, offering prayers of love and strength for every woman.

THEME TWO

A God-Conscious Mind

God is the architect of your calling—your mission, purpose, the essence of your being and life. Yet, as we navigate life, we encounter many other influences besides God's truth and love. Many of these influences can lead us away from God's truth. Through living, learning, and working, and through family, friends, and social media, we learn different ideas about life and what matters. With all of the knowledge and ideas we are exposed to, how do you keep your mind grounded in the truth?

Some knowledge points us toward God, and toward our calling, while some knowledge moves us away from God and our calling. When there is uncertainty or confusion, doubt often enters the mind. When doubt arrives, truth is often obscured. Doubt can spread, infiltrate, and weaken the powerful ability of the mind to be aligned with the highest truth.

For these next three days, we explore the origins of doubt and how to recognize and transcend it. We explore how cultivating a consciousness of God's truth empowers you to honor and bring forth the sacred purpose of the woman you are called to be.

Day 4

The Divine Pause: Exposing Doubt and Expanding Truth

For God knows that in the day you eat from it your eyes will be opened, and you will be like God, knowing good and evil.

Genesis 3:5 NASB1995

Imagine standing in front of a mirror, by yourself, no clothes, naked. There I was, fit, a college senior, working out five times a week. Friends commented on my weight loss, that perhaps I was getting too thin. Yet, when I looked in the mirror, I looked past the well-toned muscles and fixated on every single place where I thought I needed to improve. Yet, no matter how much I worked out or how many miles I jogged, this ideal of a perfect, well-toned body with completely flat abs always seemed to stay just out of my reach.

I became obsessed with eating a low-fat diet—low-fat milk, low-fat cheese, low-fat anything and everything. If I over-indulged beyond my low-fat limits, I could feel the butter, fat, cream, and every excess calorie slowly sliding through my body, transforming into fat cells. Then, I had an idea: If I never *digested* the food, then my body wouldn't take in the fat. If I ate too much, I could simply throw up the food. But...I was too squeamish to make myself vomit. And I could feel myself beginning to slide down a slippery slope. I realized that if I made myself vomit to avoid gaining weight, I might really lose control and descend into far worse problems than not being thin enough. All of this gave me pause.

Even though I never crossed the line into a full-blown eating disorder, I had a problem. My perception of myself was totally out of whack. When I looked in the mirror, I could not perceive myself clearly or accurately. My vision had become clouded. I could not appreciate myself simply as the young woman I was—fit, healthy, and happy. This obsessive standard for thinness had warped my perception. I was judging myself against an elusive, ever-shifting beauty ideal of the super-fit, fabulous, and flawless celebrities.

Insecurity gained a foothold in my mind. In that space between what I saw in the mirror and the ideal in my mind, feelings of dissatisfaction, inadequacy, and thoughts of not quite measuring up crept in. My mind leapt to dangerous places—to places of extreme self-judgment and self-criticism.

Looking back at the moment of distorted perception, it was a divine wake-up call. I was holding beliefs and thoughts in my mind that caused me to conspire against myself, to even entertain the thought of an eating disorder, risking my own health and well-being merely to stay thin. My own thoughts were leading me astray. Yet, God gives us a way forward.

For God knows that in the day you eat from it your eyes will be opened, and you will be like God, knowing good and evil.

Genesis 3:5 NASB1995

While this passage in Genesis has many interpretations, I see it as a powerful portrayal of how doubt, deception, and self-destructive thinking can lead us astray. It is also an eternal reminder of the power of our own, conscious minds to choose the highest truth. In Genesis 3:1, the serpent, the purveyor of deception and doubt, slides over to Eve and asks, "Indeed, has God said, 'You shall not eat from any tree of the garden'?"

Eve responds that God said she should not eat from that tree, lest she die. Discounting Eve's response, the serpent counters, in Genesis 3:4-5, "You surely will not die! For God knows that in the day you eat from it your eyes will be opened, and you will be like God, knowing good and evil."

Eve doubts God's instruction, entertains the deceptive thought, and eats the apple. Her eyes are then opened to perceiving good and evil, and doubt now enters her consciousness and resides in her mind. The serpent had one goal in questioning Eve: to diminish her belief, her knowledge, and her trust in God.

The Scripture shows how deceptive, self-destructive thinking operates. Once doubt grows in the mind, it weakens our trust, our faith, and our soul-deep knowing of an innate connection to God that leads us. With doubt filling the mind, the power and possibility of a mind attuned to God is greatly and dangerously diminished.

The story also shows us our own power in the face of deception. We have the conscious power and deliberate choice to hold truth and faith in our minds, and to recognize and reject doubt. We have the sacred choice to either trust God or to doubt God.

I now appreciate that moment in college, where I stood at the precipice of a dangerous eating disorder, as a divine pause. Within the sacred space of this divine pause, I learned to become more self-aware, not just of what I was doing to my body, but what was happening in my *mind.*

All the falsehoods about an "ideal" body image and my own extremely self-critical thoughts led me to a very precarious point. I recognized that I was out of alignment with my own thoughts. So I stopped weighing myself. I literally stopped getting on the scale. I needed to feel and connect with my own well-being and the truest, deepest measure of myself as the woman God created me to be, rather than a number on a scale. Waves of doubt and personal judgment came and went ... but they eventually subsided.

With time, loving myself wholly and happily became my mindset, as I truly learned to embrace me—all of me. The other thoughts—those endless, nagging doubts and false standards—started to feel inferior, wasteful, and dishonoring. Our minds hold the awesome power of choice to follow the highest thoughts of who we are and what is possible in our lives. We can choose thoughts that honor our soul, honor God, and honor our connection with God. When you pause, you have the opportunity to reflect on your thoughts, and whether it aligns with the truth of who God created you to be. You can reflect on whether or not your thoughts serve to undermine, distract, or lead you away from truth.

Whether it be thoughts that flood your mind about judging your body, or even judging your talents, gifts, and potential to do something God has called you to do, you have the power to decide. This is a sacred choice. With full faith and total trust in God, we find the clarity in our minds that enlightens and guides our path. Doubts will come. We can choose thoughts that honor and uplift. We can discard thoughts that tear down and diminish. This is not always easy. Yet, when we hear our own thoughts clearly, we can hear the truth of God.

Yet, as we navigate our decisions, we must appreciate the difference between doubt and simply not knowing something, a specific course, outcome, or how something will work out. Faith moves us forward when we do not know. While doubt creates a confusing mix of different energies, questions, and thoughts that fill and flood your mind with fear.

Reflecting on Eve, before entertaining the serpent, she had total trust in God. With full trust in God, we have clarity. We have a soul-deep knowing—a compass that directs our thoughts to God's truth. Like Eve, knowing "good and evil," we have the power to consciously *choose* what we think.

To be mindful, we must take a divine pause. There, we can sift through the doubt, find the truth, and let it expand in your mind. You can hold a powerful scripture in your mind or a sacred thought of God's vision, love, and concept of you. You can ask yourself whether the thought leads you toward or away from your calling, your truth, and the image of the woman God created you to be. Our gifts, our light, our lives, and callings are much too powerful, precious, and much-needed blessings to be sabotaged by doubt. Gratefully, God gives you the sacred and powerful choice to choose the highest thoughts, His truth, and the image of the woman God called you to be.

Devotion

Thank you, God, for the enduring truth of Your word. Thank you for the wisdom You have given me and the power of my mind to seek Your truth. I pray for Your continual guidance of my thoughts. When doubt, fears, or confusion come, please lead me to the purest, highest, and clearest truth. Lead me away from all that does not honor You and lead me toward Your light. Thank you, God, for giving me the power to choose You with all of my heart, all of my soul, and all of my mind.

Reflection

Reflect on your most challenging times. Did thoughts of uncertainty, doubt, or fear come? What were you thinking and believing? Write down all that comes up.

Now, imagine what God would say to you in those moments. What truth do you hear? Write down all that you hear. Speak these truths out loud.

Relfect on what you wrote above. Now, set your own powerful affirmation. What truths do you know in your soul? What beliefs and thoughts can you affirm to lead you through doubt? What beliefs and thoughts can you affirm to move you toward God and your ultimate calling?

Write your own devotion here.

Read it aloud, stand up and let the strength of God's love sink deep into your soul.

Group Discussion

Begin with each person sharing their devotion and reflections on Day 4. What can you share, if anything, that you may have had fear, doubt, or confusion about? Allow this to be a safe place to simply be heard without the need to advise or instruct. Ask each person: What truth can you hold in your mind as you navigate challenges? What false beliefs, if any, that do not honor you and God, can you let go? Close with an affirming group prayer of encouragement, clarity, and strength.

Day 5

To Garden Your Consciousness and Plant Your Intention

"But the seed in the good soil, these are the ones who have heard the word in an honest and good heart, hold it fast, and bear fruit with perseverance."

Luke 8:15 NASB1995

People who know me know I used to LOVE Oprah. I used to tell people, "I can't stop now!" as I hurried across the Quad, picked up my food, and made my way to my college dorm room in time to watch *The Oprah Winfrey Show*. My grandma knew how much I loved Oprah too. And one year, she gave me a wonderful Christmas gift: in addition to her legendary fruit cake, a subscription to *O Magazine*! I so much enjoyed curling up on the couch with the magazine in Grandma's living room, with our beloved cat Rocky, sipping on a cup of coffee. I would immediately flip to the end of the magazine to read Oprah's column, "What I Know for Sure." I loved the distillation of her wisdom and this one particular message: the power of intention.

I admired Oprah, how she used her voice and platform with authority, purpose, and impact. Reading her magazine, I wanted to absorb some of her wisdom and connect it with my own desire to use my voice and creativity for a meaningful purpose. The concept of beginning everything with intention—a conscious, willful, mental determination and decision about each and every action—stuck with me. What I admired in her work did not happen randomly, by circumstances, or by any kind of luck, but flowed through intention. The very magazine I was holding was the result of intention.

Intention, the powerful force and potential of the mind, sets processes, actions, and thoughts in motion. Intention, the power of conscious decision, flows from awareness and clarity. We have the power to be intentional about what we think and what we create. Intention gives birth to possibilities. These possibilities, when we tap into our soul, flow from the vast, expansive force of the intentions God has ordained. We gain a glimpse of the unlimited intention of God in the parable of the sower.

"Now the parable is this: the seed is the word of God."
Luke 8:11 NASB1995

The seed is the Word of God, the truth that we can choose to receive into our heart, mind, and soul, that God grows within us. The seed holds the infinite potential of all that can be born and made manifest in our lives when we receive God's word. A seed, by its nature, carries the intention of the Creator, carrying vast possibilities of creation, yet, requiring the soil, the *soul*, to be planted within. While we see the potential in the power of the Word of God, the parable also makes clear the necessity of our intention to receive it.

12 *"Those beside the road are those who have heard; then the devil comes and takes away the word from their heart, so that they will not believe and be saved.*
13 *Those on the rocky soil are those who, when they hear, receive the word with joy; and these have no firm root; they believe for a while, and in time of temptation fall away.*

14 The seed which fell among the thorns, these are the ones who have heard, and as they go on their way they are choked with worries and riches and pleasures of this life, and bring no fruit to maturity."
Luke 8:12-14 NASB1995

All of these things—whether it be temptation, doubt, or deception—can enter our minds and take away the power of the Word. Whether it be stress, worry, discord, or simply the busyness of life, our minds and lives can be so distracted that the power of the Word does not have the opportunity to germinate, settle in, and grow roots in our soul. This parable from Jesus is about believing the Word of God and accepting salvation. Yet, it also shows the state of our consciousness, our minds, and the power of our intention to choose.

Imagine what the worries would have been when this passage was first recorded. Today, the context of our lives is very different. Our lives can be bombarded and burdened with various pursuits, complications, pleasures, and distractions. With a single tap on the phone or a swipe on any social media app, we can be immediately flooded with thousands of ideas, opinions, and activities, all of which consume valuable space and energy in the mind and can take our minds and our daily lives in many different, and often unintended, directions.

When I moved into my home, I unexpectedly found myself very free of mental distractions. I was so happy to finally settle in, but there was one major wrinkle. I had no cable television! And this was before I even had a Smart Phone. It would take two weeks before the installation could be completed. Within that time, my habits changed drastically. There was no turning on the cable news as I got dressed in the morning. And I couldn't even watch Oprah! I saw no celebrity stories, no images of violence, no political drama, not even the softer, feel-good stories. I didn't even bother to listen to the radio.

Within the space of my home, silence reigned. At first, it felt odd. But I slowly noticed that I could hear my own thoughts more clearly, without the constant chatter, interruptions, flood of information, and other voices. I found the silence to be a powerful tool and the much-needed space to weed out the mental clutter. I began to relish the silence, to cherish the quiet space where I could be intentional with my own thoughts, with a new depth and clarity.

For me, to hear God is to remove the chatter and open the mind expansively. And, in that space, to consciously plant powerful intentions. Like a mind free of distraction, the parable in Luke 8:15 ends with an image of the good soil—a receptive soul and a clear mind, fertile with the Word of God.

"But the seed in the good soil, these are the ones who have heard the word in an honest and good heart, and hold it fast, and bear fruit with perseverance."

In "good soil," the consciousness and the mind are free, clear, and receptive. The good soil is a fertile mind, an open heart, and a receptive soul. The Word of God, its truth, power, and potentiality, takes root and bears fruit in our lives. We can set the intention to hear God's truth above all else—what you know God is leading you to be, do and bring forth in your life. Yet, we must do this with purpose and perseverance. We must intentionally weed the garden of our minds. Pull out, discard, and disengage what is not fruitful. As what you plant grows, you must intentionally choose what you will plant. You can plant worry and grow confusion. You can plant love and grow compassion. You can plant powerful ideas, and the Word of God, and let it yield amazing possibilities.

When I think of those special moments in the blessed company of Grandma and my cat Rocky while reading Oprah's magazine, I appreciate the fertile soil of those times. Grandma herself planted something within me—her love, belief, and affirmation of my ideas of the future. I had no way of knowing then that I would one day capture our precious moments in my writing of this very book so many years later. Yet, her belief was a seed that grew within me. And as Oprah has said in the past, and what I know for sure, "God could dream a bigger dream than what I could ever dream."

Finally, after two weeks, I got my cable television turned on. Yet, I held on to the sacred gift that the silence had created—the intentional space to consciously focus on what I hold in my mind. As planters of intention, we weed out what is unfruitful and pour energy into what matters most. You have the sacred choice to plant intentional thoughts, to enrich the fertile soil of your mind, and receive divine sunlight onto all that God has entrusted within you.

To keep your mind grounded, focused, and clear is a continual and constant act. You have the powerful decision, thought by thought, intention by intention, to let your mind, your soul, and indeed your entire life bear the fruit and the glory God has given you. In that space, you open to the blessing of God's richness and possibilities to manifest abundantly—growing and overflowing in your life.

Devotion

Dear God, thank you for the power of Your word and the possibilities You have planted in my soul. I pray for Your wisdom to guide my every thought and decision. I pray that I will be a faithful steward of all that You have entrusted in me. Please strengthen my intention and let Your truth be the compass that leads my mind, soul, and life. In Jesus's name, I pray, Amen.

Reflection

Allow yourself 10 minutes to reflect on today's message. What thoughts arose? Write freely about all that comes up. How would you describe the fertile soil of your mind? What thoughts are you allowing in? What conscious intentions are you holding?

Reflect on what matters most to you now and ask God for guidance. What thoughts, if any, can you weed out? What is the most powerful intention you can set now?

Set a powerful mantra to ground your intention. What words or Scripture can you use to affirm your intention and guide your thoughts? Repeat the affirmation out loud and feel it in your heart and mind.

Write your own devotion here.

Read it aloud and allow it to penetrate deeply into your heart and mind.

Group Discussion

Begin with each person sharing their devotion and reflections on Day 5. Ask everyone to share: What intention do you have now? Allow this to be a safe space for all to be heard with appreciation. What actions can you take to affirm, strengthen and act on that intention? Ask each person to share an affirmation for another person—to positively sow into another person by affirming their intentions. Close with a group prayer of grace, clarity, and affirmation of your highest intentions.

Day 6

To Meditate on Truth and Enlighten Possibilities

Finally, brethren, whatever is true, whatever is honorable, whatever is right, whatever is pure, whatever is lovely, whatever is of good repute, if there is any excellence and if anything worthy of praise, dwell on these things.

Philippians 4:8 NASB1995

It was a shining moment, literally. I was sitting on the stage with bright lights shining on me, and I could barely see the audience sitting in the darkened auditorium. I was part of a production of Eve Ensler's *The Vagina Monologues*. I was portraying a young woman, reflecting on her memories from ages 3 to 16 years old, who had been sexually abused in her childhood.

Preparing for the part, I had to memorize every line. For each section of the script, my rehearsal partner helped me learn by repeating each line seven times. Chrissa, the director, pushed me to explore the feelings and depth of meaning in every word. She asked me to imagine how I would feel and speak at each age and how I would feel to be betrayed. She asked me to imagine feeling those painful memories as I retold her story. I studied each word, deeply imagining this young woman, and absorbed her words closely and intimately.

On the night of the performance, as I spoke her story, I felt connected as though her message was real. She was flowing through me, as though I started to recede, becoming a conduit, and her voice came shining through. After the final show, as cast members, friends, and family gathered, I spoke to the producer who had played the music throughout our performances. He told me that his wife was moved to tears during my performance, hearing the story of the young survivor. I can only imagine what touched her. Something came through the performance, in that moment, that touched her heart. By giving voice to what was painful, shameful, and concealed, there was light. The survivor's words now rang out in the packed auditorium in the full light of God. All those rehearsals were well worth it—the soul of her story came shining through to touch the hearts and souls of others.

The practice of studying, learning, and honoring her words so deeply was like meditation. To meditate on the words is to dwell deeply with them, and absorb them, to convey a greater meaning to the audience. In the performance, a brighter light and spirit emerged, greater than the words on the page, and greater than my own acting. The performance became the conduit through which a greater spiritual energy flowed and overflowed. Preparing for this performance was very much like studying and meditating on God's words. Where with deep study, a greater energy flows through you.

When I meditate on and absorb God's words, I find deeper meaning and connect with truth. Meditating on God's words, deeply and profoundly, lets the truth seep into our minds. We can feel it, ponder it, hold it, and let it come through our own voices and works so that the light of God shines through our lives and touches others.

Finally, brethren, whatever is true, whatever is honorable, whatever is right, whatever is pure, whatever is lovely, whatever is of good repute, if there is any excellence and if anything worthy of praise, dwell on these things.
Philippians 4:8 NASB1995

To dwell is to abide in, focus on, absorb, concentrate, ponder, and behold. To dwell is to let your heart and let your mind meditate on and inhabit all that is true, right, pure, lovely, and worthy of praise. Yet, to dwell is not simply for the consciousness of your mind, it is a pathway to peace and the presence of God. The verse continues:

The things you have learned and received and heard and see in me, practice these things, and the God of peace will be with you.
Philippians 4:9 NASB1995

As we practice dwelling on what is good and as we make the necessary space for God's truth in our minds, we feel the presence and the peace of God. Cultivating this mindset is powerful for our own well-being. Imagine your mind being filled with peace and possibilities. When we deeply attune our minds to the highest good and God's truth, we become actors on our own stage, allowing all of our talents to serve His purposes. God's purpose, who we are called to touch, love, and impact, flows through us when we set our minds on God, meditate, and deeply absorb what is good, powerful, and true. In this way, as an actor reads a script, we become powerful conduits in the creation of God's ever-evolving story.

God endows each and every one of us with unique talents, inclinations, and desires. When we set our minds to meditate deeply on God's word, on what is true and excellent, the flow of God's grace moves in and through us with infinite energy, creating endless possibilities. This continual attunement, practice, and purposeful decision to meditate on the highest good invites God's grace to flow through our lives.

After the final performance of the play, the director asked the entire cast to come backstage. She put tremendous time and effort into rehearsing with each actress individually so that we could all masterfully deliver our parts. Bringing us together one last time, she shared a message that I remember dearly. She presented each cast member with the framed words of Marianne Williamson:

"Our deepest fear is not that we are inadequate. Our deepest fear is that we are powerful beyond measure. It is our light, not our darkness that most frightens us."

We had come together, a group of women investing our time and passion, to raise our voices to amplify the stories of other women. Chrissa gave us markers and asked each woman to sign the glass of each person's framed poem. She left us with an indelible message—we had accomplished what we set out to do. We had magnified the voices and stories of survivors. Yet, she also asked us to remember our own power—to let our own gifts, talents, and light brilliantly and boldly shine.

Before the performance, I rehearsed. A lot. But, I also prayed. I prayed for the work we were doing, for it to be used for a mighty purpose, and for it to be a blessing to others. This very act—attuning deeply into the mind, setting the highest intentions, and praying for your talent to touch others in a positive way—lets the power of God work. Whenever we watch a play, a movie, or have a conversation that deeply touches our soul, we feel this power. When you meditate on the sublime truth of God's words, all that is good, true, excellent, and possible, you truly become a conduit of God's grace.

To dwell with God is to hold a sacred consciousness in your mind. We have an awesome power to dwell on the highest good in the fertile consciousness of our minds. To let what is good, powerful, blessed, and true deepen and expand our consciousness, we open our lives to let God's glory shine through. This sacred consciousness allows us to be a blessing to many others. To meditate deeply on what is possible, you connect with God's grandest possibilities and the power and potential of your calling. To dwell in the highest good, to dwell with the Lord, you tap into all that God has created and called you to do. Wherever you sit or stand in life, whoever you are called to touch, the power and light of your spirit is a much-needed blessing. Let your mind dwell in your highest possibilities, the highest calling God has for you, and let your awesome, blessed light brilliantly and beautifully shine.

Devotion

Dear God, thank you for Your continual presence and everlasting peace. I pray that You lead and direct my mind to all that is good, powerful, and true. I pray that You open my mind to hear the infinite wisdom in Your words. Please show me the pathways, the people, and the opportunities to fulfill the calling You have ordained for me. I pray that all You have entrusted in my soul and life will be in service to Your purposes. I pray that Your grace, love, blessing, and light will flow in my life. With abiding gratitude and love, I pray. Thank you, God. Amen.

Reflection

Imagine your mind as a completely blank slate. No problems, no joys. There is total peace and space. Now ask yourself: What one thing matters most to you right now? Now, returning to the Scripture, ask yourself what is true, honorable, right, pure, lovely, of good repute, excellence, worthy of praise, about this *one* thing? Write down all that comes up.

Reflect on what you wrote above. Take 10 minutes to meditate and dwell on your words. How did it feel, in your mind, to contemplate the highest good of what matters most to you?

Now, turn your mind to God. How can what matters most to you be a blessing in your life and to others? What guidance do you seek from God?

Write your own devotion here.

Read it aloud and allow it to absorb deeply into your heart, soul, and mind.

Group Discussion

Begin with each person sharing their devotion and reflections on Day 6. Reflecting on Days 4 and 5 as well, how have you deepened the awareness and intentionality of your own thoughts? Where have you been successful? Where have you struggled? Share strategies for edifying this mental practice of cultivating a God-conscious mind. Ask each person to share what matters most to them. End with prayers upholding each person's intentions and asking for God's grace and blessings to flow to you and through you.

THEME THREE

Baptism: To Enter a Covenant with God

We enter into a covenant with God, a sacred agreement, when we choose God with our souls. Baptism is an outward demonstration of the covenant with God when you accept Jesus Christ as your Lord and Savior. For various religious traditions and beliefs, coming to God does not necessarily require the act of a water baptism. Yet, coming to God is always a covenant in the soul. In making this decision, we come into agreement with God to accept all that God is, to trust God, to be led by God, to be touched and transformed by the Spirit of God, every day of our lives for the rest of our lives. In this sacred relationship, we open up our souls to fulfill, embody and express the sacred purposes God has ordained in our lives.

For these next three days, we explore three dimensions of how our souls come into a personal covenant with God—through prayer, through baptism, and through soulful surrender. In deepening and honoring the holy relationship with God, you dwell deeper in the transformative power of God, deeper into the very purpose, and deeper into the very soul of the woman God has called you to be.

Day 7

The Power of Sacred Prayer

Then you will call upon Me and come and pray to Me, and I will listen to you. You will seek Me and find Me when you search for Me with all your heart.

Jeremiah 29:12-13 NASB1995

My grandmother first taught me to pray. During the summers while we were growing up, my brother, cousin, and I would spend weeks at my grandparent's home in Gloucester, Virginia—"the country," as we called it. After hours of working in Grandpa's garden, swimming at the beach, or roaming the area with a dog named Scruffy, we would be exhausted. Every night as I got ready for bed, Grandma would come into my room and say, "It's time to say your prayers." Grandma, always so full of life with gleaming eyes, would kneel down with me beside my bed. We closed our eyes, lifted our hands, and said the prayer:

"Now I lay me down to sleep, I pray the Lord my soul to keep, and if I die before I wake, I pray the Lord my soul to take. Amen."

Then, Grandma gave me a special bonus; she told me I can now pray for anyone I wanted to pray for. I launched into overtime and prayed for everyone! I prayed for my mom and dad, and my other grandma and Pop-Pop, Uncle Darnee, my aunt and uncle, our neighbors, friends, and anyone we visited that day. I was praying to the Protector of the world, so I could not leave anyone out. I felt a sense of joyful, loving power that I could pray for people and that God would bless them.

Those moments of prayer were special. Praying before bed made me feel like sleep was a great mystery where God was with me and watching over me. Praying to God to look over my loved ones and keep them safe made me feel close with everyone and close with God. Through prayer, Grandma taught me how to enter into a personal relationship with God. She taught me to open my heart in prayer, to be responsible, and to care for others. This gave me a sense of power. Even as a little girl, through prayer, I could speak directly to God—entering into a realm of love and compassion without boundary. Praying with my whole heart, I believed God was listening to me and that His blessings would come to pass.

Even though prayer was a constant for me, in my early 20s and living on my own, I moved away from attending church. Growing into my own sense of self, I disagreed with some of the religious teachings, especially about the roles of women. For some reason, I felt the church was a place for perfect people—people who knew exactly what God required and were living their lives in total agreement with God's word. With my many questions, and being single, dating, and embarking on my own path, I didn't quite feel that I *fit* in church. Church seemed like a place for married couples, families, and older people living established lives according to a Christian pattern. I needed to find my own answers about religion and God, and I felt this pull to explore outside of the church.

I explored all things New Age, spiritual, and everything in between. I went up and down the New Age aisle in many now-defunct bookstores, plunging into my own search for meaning and purpose. I learned a lot about thought, matter, and manifesting. A common theme was that we could create whatever we desire through thought, energy, gratitude, and connection to a higher source. And that we can experience whatever we wish in life, relationships, and success. Yet, still, something was missing.

There was only me, with all my New Age tools, trying to make things happen and charting my own course ... alone. Yet, I hungered for more. I needed something more solid, bigger, grander, the ultimate, unshakeable answer to purpose, beyond what I could manifest or desire in my own thinking and searching. Even though I learned that I had the power to bring anything into existence, I hungered for something at the soul level. I realized God was missing—the God that anchored and oriented my soul. The purpose and meaning I sought led me back to my own, now much deeper, even more personal relationship with God. My soul was longing for true communion that transcends the self and fulfills a deeper meaning beyond my own desires. I felt my soul hungering for a true connection with God that would guide, connect, and provide the very foundation for my purpose in life.

In prayer with God, even while I was soul-searching, it was never just *me*. It was always me with God, even if I felt like I was alone. God, the Creator who knit the world and every human being together, was always there. During the most challenging and soul-searching times, I prayed, just like I did as a little girl with my Grandma. And as an adult living in my own apartment, I still started my prayers with, *"Now I lay me down to sleep, I pray the Lord my soul to keep."*

I was seeking God, who I had been communing with for a very long time, to be the Lord, the deeper purpose, the truth, and the guiding force of my life. Through all my soul-searching, exploring, studying, and reading, I came back to needing the unfailing love and power of God to be at the center of my life.

I heard a pastor once say that God plants within human beings a hunger for a spiritual connection with God. That hunger had been pulling me, driving my soul-seeking for years. Like the physical body hungers for nourishment and affection, the soul hungers for connection with God. Late nights, watching television evangelists preach, they often closed with an invitation to accept Christ. In my living room, I would pray along with them, "Jesus, Come into my heart."

Then you will call upon Me and come and pray to Me, and I will listen to you. You will seek Me and find Me when you search for Me with all your heart.
Jeremiah 29:12-13 NASB1995

I had searched and searched, explored and explored. Now, I was calling on God to give me personal diretion. And, I found God—in my own prayers. Prayer is powerful. Prayer grows a connection in your heart to God. In this sacred communion with the Divine, with the simple act of speaking His name, raising your voice to meet the presence of God, you step into a new realm. A realm of grace, love, and connection with the Almighty that fills your soul.

In the act of prayer, I was believing in God. In prayer, I knew God was real, alive, and hearing my every word. I did not know it at the time, but moving away from church and seeking my own answers was not a rejection. It was a path for me to find an even deeper, more powerful, and more personal relationship with God. Prayer was my steady companion, my sacred connection. This path led me gradually back into church, back to reading my Bible with an open heart, and back to praying to God to receive the answers I most needed.

Prayer is a covenant that God gives us. When earnestly seeking God with your heart, coming in gratitude, coming with questions, coming in need, however we come, God hears us. In prayer, with your heart wide open, your soul finds and leads the way.

No matter where you are in your life or on your journey, whether you have come to God, are growing with God, have accepted Christ, or are still questioning, God gives you the power of prayer. Prayer steadies your journey and always illuminates your path. Prayer ushers us into the presence of wisdom, love, direction, truth, and all that God has endowed in the purposes of our lives. With a genuine desire to seek and to know God, God gives us a way. God gives you the sacred power of prayer.

Devotion

Dear God, I open my heart fully to You and will pray to You, in every matter, for every cause, throughout all the days of my life. I am humbled and awed by Your eternal presence in every moment of my existence. I thank you for the sacred power of prayer, that I can seek You and share everything in my heart, mind, and soul. I pray that our connection endures and grows and that it guides and leads me every step of my life. I am eternally grateful that I can call on You, that I am heard, and that You are with me always. With an open heart, I pray. Thank you, God. Amen.

Reflection

Reflect on your relationship with God. What weighs on your heart, mind, or soul most deeply right now? What do you most need to bring before God in prayer? Write down all that comes up.

Now, consider your prayer life. When and where do you pray? How do you feel and what are you believing as you pray? How can you deepen and expand the power of prayer in your life? Be specific as possible.

Take 5 minutes and meditate on the Scripture for Day 7, feeling it in your heart. Write down all you hear, feel, and think. Reflect on what you most need to bring to God now and speak it in prayer.

Write your own devotion here.

Feel the love in your heart, focus on the love of God, and say your devotion as a prayer.

Group Discussion

Begin with a prayer and gratitude to God for bringing the group together. Ask each person to share their reflections on Day 7 and what is on their hearts now. How can you deepen your prayer life? Share what works well for you. What, if anything, have you not brought before God? Consider: How might sharing this with God be beneficial? Conclude with each woman sharing her devotion. Close with a prayer, lifting up what is on the heart of each woman to God.

Day 8

The Power of Accepting Jesus Christ

"Truly, truly, I say to you, he who believes has eternal life."
John 6:47 NASB1995

My mother kept asking me to come to church. She upped the ante by promising me brunch afterward—Jesus and waffles!—so I finally came. We sat toward the back of the church, beside the aisle. As the sermon ended, the minister invited anyone who wanted to receive Christ to come forward. A heavy longing filled my heart. I had been laboring in a stressed-out cycle of work, graduate school, and very little sleep. Something touched me that day. The peace, the spirit in the sanctuary, gave me a feeling of comfort and relief, and I had this strong desire to just let go.

Tears welled up in my body, and a rising urge to get up and walk forward. But I held back the tears and held on tightly to that pew. I knew that if I stood up, I would fall apart and crumble into a heap of tears. I thought of how I would appear, surrendering to this overwhelming feeling, completely losing any semblance of composure I possessed. I felt like I would be falling into something I did not understand. I did not know what I was stepping forward into and was not sure what would happen to me when I got to the altar. I didn't want to fall apart. So I sat still. And I just held on to the pew.

Church used to be a familiar place for me. My grandfather, a master builder and general contractor, literally built the East Capitol Street Church of Christ in Washington, DC, where I grew up going to church. Grandpa was an elder, and every Sunday, we went to church. I admit it, as a little girl during church, I frequently thought about what I was going to eat after the service was over.

I loved when we got to the final closing song, *"Blest be the tie that binds our hearts in Christian love."* I knew that song by heart and loved singing it. Church was over, and I was free to go! Still, I would watch baptisms in awe as the minister pulled back the curtains and dunked the person in the water. After church, my brother and I would sneak around to the back room behind the pulpit and peer into the mini pool. Yet, my mom believed that children should make their own decision about being baptized, and she never questioned me about that decision.

During the summers, my brother, Kenan, and I spent a lot of time with Grandma and Grandpa at their house in Virginia, and we would attend the Gloucester Church of Christ, which my grandfather also built. Grandpa, 6'3" tall and weighing over 230 pounds, never told me a lot to do—except to wake up at five o'clock in the morning to work in the garden. My brother, cousin, and I would dig rows of potatoes and pick string beans. We were in work clothes, we were hot and sweating in the summer sun, but we loved Grandpa. And He loved us. Grandpa called me "Queen." I loved hearing his voice in the mornings when I walked into the kitchen. I beamed and smiled as Grandpa greeted me, "Hello, Queen."

Decades later, my Grandpa remained strong in heart, but not in body. After valiantly battling prostate cancer for three years, his broad, tall frame became thin, frail, and weak. I tended to his hands, massaging and rubbing hand cream on them to soothe the rough skin. I held his hands—hands that had worked so hard his entire life. At the end, his body gave way, and his spirit moved on. My mother was there with him in his final moments—and he shared a message that etched in my soul.

Before my beloved grandfather died, he said, "Make sure Konyka and Kenan know Christ." His final words felt like truth—the sum total of what he believed in his life, his purpose, his legacy, and what he wanted to impart to those he dearly loved. Through 84 years of life and all the knowledge and wisdom gained through raising a family, building homes and churches, having lived through challenging times that could make one embittered with racism and injustice, he exuded love, generosity, and an incredible fullness of faith. His final message to me—know Christ—hit me hard. I think that my grandfather, in his last moments while his spirit still had a voice, wanted to impart a message for my soul, one of enduring love. *Accept Christ.*

Like my mother, who allowed me the freedom to make my own decision about baptism, he also gave me the space to decide. His final message—to know Christ for ourselves—touched my soul, and I received Grandpa's words. Knowing Christ is ultimately what matters most in this lifetime.

I studied the Bible to know Jesus more deeply in my own way. Jesus embodied concern for all human souls: His love, the miracles, the healing, wisdom, forgiveness, and the ultimate commitment to point everyone to God. His undying mission that we would not die in our sins gave humanity a way to achieve salvation through His life. Jesus's commitment to the advancement of love for all souls is like no other mission, expression of love, or embodiment of spiritual truth I have ever witnessed or experienced. The conviction of his love seared into my heart. Yet, the end of his earthly life struck me profoundly.

Knowing that he would be crucified, Jesus refused to deny his deity. To be so concerned with the souls of humanity, despite the barbaric cruelty inflicted on him, and to still speak to God Almighty, I could find no earthly reason why any human being would endure the torture, suffer the crucifixion, and still cry out to God:

Then said Jesus, "Father, forgive them; for they know not what they do."
Luke 23:34 KJV

The love of Christ, displayed on the Cross, captured me. Jesus cried out to God, interceding for our souls, in His last few words for all of humankind. This is the greatest love of all—the love of our souls for all eternity. The love that had anchored my grandfather, the love of Christ that he wanted me to know.

I continued to study and pray and made the decision to accept Christ as my Lord and Savior. I had always trusted in God's providence, believed God was everywhere, and I was certain of God's infinite love and power. God had always been with me, watching, and I believe, *waiting*. I had just never said *yes*, completely, and consciously, to entering into this covenant of my soul with Christ, for Jesus Christ to be the center, the rock, and the guide of all my life.

Thinking back to the day in church, when I held on to the pew, was when I first felt the pull of Christ on my heart. Even though I didn't stand up and walk to the altar, that pull, that knocking on my heart, never left me. If anything, it *led* me. It led me through making my way to the Lord, navigating my own experiences, exploring religion, studying, listening, contemplating, and praying. Over the years, I got close to God in my soul. Yet, when I decided *no more seeking*, the resistance gave way, and I chose God fully with all of my heart, mind, soul, and life. I decided to be baptized.

Every part of me believes and knows that God loves the soul of every single person. Jesus Christ shows us the way of love and truth and invites us to come into the most profound, eternal relationship with God. As my family allowed me a sacred space to choose, I believe we all must navigate our own paths. Yet, know, wherever you are, Jesus Christ is with you. Pray to Jesus, call on, give grace, say thank you, ask for healing, help, or say to Him—*Yes, I need You. Come into my heart.* Like my Grandpa, what I know for sure—know Christ.

Devotion

Thank you, God, for your son, Jesus Christ. Thank you for His resurrected Spirit, whose love we can call on every moment of our lives. Thank you for His sacrifice, transformative power, healing, and the path He shows us to You. May the love of Christ guide me, and touch me, every step of my life. May the character and truth of Christ lead me in the woman you have called me to be. May the love of Christ be magnified through me and all of my purposes. In Jesus's name, I pray, Amen.

Reflection

Reflect for a moment on your relationship with Jesus Christ. Where are you on your spiritual journey? What, if anything, are you seeking? What do you most need now? Write down all that comes up.

Consider for a moment if there are any hindrances and obstacles that block your relationship with God. Look within yourself as well. What are those obstacles, if any? How could a deeper relationship with God help you to overcome any challenges?

Take a few minutes and reflect on God and Jesus Christ. What do you know for sure? How does your knowledge of Jesus Christ inform and guide your life?

Write your own devotion here.

Allow it to absorb deeply into your heart and soul. Say it out loud in a prayer.

Group Discussion

Begin with each person sharing their devotion and reflections on Day 8. What does it mean to truly accept Jesus Christ? Let this be an open discussion, with no judgment or pressure. Ask each person to share (if willing) where they are on their path with God. Share your feelings, thoughts, and questions. If applicable, what led you to accept Christ? How has accepting Christ impacted you? End with prayer in gratitude to Jesus Christ and lift up each woman on her journey.

Day 9

The Power of Soulful Surrender

"Abide in Me, and I in you. As the branch cannot bear fruit of itself unless it abides in the vine, so neither can you unless you abide in Me."

John 15:4 NASB1995

On Wednesday night Bible Study, I stood up from the pew and walked forward for the altar call to be baptized. I was clear, determined, and I was ready. I had no idea what to expect, yet I was open to all that would come. I put on a robe and an old-school white swimming cap with a chin strap. Entering the baptismal pool, the minister led me down three steps into the cool, waist-high water. The curtains parted, and the church members were revealed, sitting in the pews and looking at me. It was a moment 38 years in the making.

The minister asked me did I believe in Jesus Christ and did I repent of my sins. I answered *Yes* and *Yes*. I stated my belief in the death, burial, and resurrection of Christ. The minister then baptized me in the name of Jesus Christ. He dipped me backward and submerged me completely underwater. For a second, I felt like he gave me an extra shake under that water to make sure the faith took hold, then he brought me back up again. Baptized into the body of Christ! I emerged from the water a new creature.

After I got dressed, I joined the church members in a closing prayer circle. Hugs and warmth oozed from everyone. I felt surrounded by and uplifted in pure love. When I got home that evening, I stopped on the step at my front door, gazed into the night sky, and watched an airplane fly by. This moment, my long walk to Christ had finally arrived. I looked up and said, "Thank you, God."

Before I was baptized, I wondered what exactly would be different afterward. I wondered if there would be any real change in me or my life after being submerged in the baptismal waters. Coming to Christ was a very conscious, wholehearted decision. I chose Christ as an adult woman with lots of life experience, big goals, and ambitious plans. Now, I was stepping into the great unknown—beyond the realm of all I had known, to trust God with all my soul. Accepting Christ, I committed all of who I am to serve God, and I asked Jesus to show me the way. Yet, I still did not know what it would mean to truly make Christ the Lord of my life. The next morning, I got the first hint of the change that would come.

When I woke up, to my surprise, I *still* felt refreshed. The night before, I had emerged refreshed from the baptismal pool. As a swimmer, I am accustomed to feeling refreshed after getting out of the water. But that baptismal water was different—it was the purest, most cleansing water I have ever felt. It was as though I was washed deeply, over and through me, inside and out, with an overflowing joy permeating every fiber of my being. I felt refreshed, renewed all the way down to the cellular level.

For days afterward, I felt joyous, whole, and grounded in peace. Something inside of me *clicked*. I felt like a glue was in my being that made all of me click into place, as though my soul and experiences came purposefully together. Prior to the baptism, I felt like I had been functioning fine, but once plugged into God, I felt a *flow*. Like a fountain connected to water, I could feel the source flowing through me. I felt like my soul had found its home.

Indeed, something was *different* after being baptized. In this mysterious union of the soul and covenant with God in the act of baptism, I felt connected in my soul as I never had before. There is this great mystery: We cannot hold God, touch or see God, nor even our own souls. Yet, the Spirit is a real force, beyond the working of the rational mind, where the soul resides with the body. Now, baptized into the *body* of Christ, our souls *abide* in Christ.

"Abide in Me, and I in you. As the branch cannot bear fruit of itself unless it abides in the vine, so neither can you unless you abide in Me."

John 15:4 NASB1995

I had chosen to surrender my soul and my life to Christ. To do so is to *abide in* Christ. To abide is to dwell in the Spirit of Christ and for Christ to dwell in me. That overflowing, refreshed, joyful feeling was the first hint, that yes, something would be very different. The "click" that I felt was the next hint. My sense of feeling like my soul was at home. Yes, that was, indeed, the feeling of abiding in Christ.

Accepting Christ was a choice—not to just believe and accept His teachings, but to be transformed by Jesus Christ. A choice to let His powerful Spirit touch me, lead me, and change me. I could feel a very real connection to Jesus Christ, a connection that also changed my sight.

While I always was a very humanitarian-minded person, after my baptism, I felt a subtle change, as though I was seeing through a wider, brighter lens of love. My sight shifted as though scales fell off of my eyes. I was seeing Spirit, even more clearly, this underlying connection of all souls that transcended race, age, nationality, and gender. The love of Christ emboldened my vision, as I was truly seeing all people as fellow souls, brothers, and sisters in Christ. I felt the transcendent power of agape love and felt even more compelled to share loving kindness with neighbors, family, and people with whom I crossed paths, yet did not even know.

While the refreshed feeling subsided after several days, a stronger internal commitment emerged. To abide in Christ is a total surrender. In surrender, we invite God to be at the center of everything. Truly, to abide in Christ is to find purpose in Christ. Without this connection of the branch to the vine, like the soul to Christ, there is no fruit—nothing can be produced, nothing can be manifest. To abide in Christ is to let your entire life purpose and your entire foundation be transformed. Holding any aspect of my life apart from Christ no longer made sense. I had felt the flow, and the flow was real. I wanted to be fully connected, transformed, and led by that flow.

I shifted in purpose. The new me, the new surrendered woman, became purposefully resolved to let God's love flow through all my life. To let all of who I am, and my life purpose, be led by Spirit. While my job did not change, *I did*. I felt a deeper meaning, as though abiding in Christ, somehow and some way, will transform every aspect of my life. This is an ongoing act of surrender—to lift up every aspect of my being, all of me, to God.

This surrender felt like power. Not power over anyone or anything, nor an ego-driven power. This was the power, the force, and the energy of feeling God, seeing God work in and through my life. I came to this sublime yet simple truth: With my soul attuned to God, *all things are possible*. Truly, and only with God, are *all* things possible. And I wanted to experience *all* that was possible. I had no concept of what would unfold in the months and years to come. Yet, I knew that asking Christ to dwell and abide in me would be a blessed, sacred, and powerful journey.

To be baptized, to enter into a covenant, in a sacred relationship with God is a sacred choice. This is a highly personal decision you make in your own conscience. It is to step into the unknown, into a trust of the Lord that always holds you. It is a surrender—a total invitation. There is no place that Christ is not welcomed. And no place that you hold back. Every part of you is enveloped by and touched by Christ. This is a relationship of a lifetime. Within this sacred covenant, you become a part of the blessed vine and bear fruit as you are called by God to do.

Devotion

Thank you, God, for the Spirit that washes over my heart, mind, soul, and every aspect of my being and life. I lift all of me to You and invite You in, this day and every day. May Your love grow within me and lead me. Thank you for all that You have given me, every gift, talent, and desire. Let it all abide in You and be lifted for Your blessed and mighty purposes. Where there is a separation between us, I invite You in. Touch me, transform me and change me. May I abide always in Your loving presence. In Jesus's name, I pray, Amen.

Reflection

Surrender. Bring it all to Christ. Reflect deeply on the Scripture for Day 9. Scan your heart and mind for anything you need to bring to Christ. What comes to mind? Write this down. Focus on this. Invite Christ in and pray for this now.

Reflect on what you wrote above. Go even deeper. Now, give it over to Christ. Imagine feeling Christ move into and completely fill your heart. What comes into your mind, your heart, and your spirit? Write down all that you hear.

Reflect on your relationship with God. Wherever you are. How can the relationship with God become even more powerful so that God flows in and through you constantly? Ponder this deeply and write down what you receive.

Write your own devotion here.

Allow it to sink deeply into your heart and soul. Speak it as a prayer and invitation to Christ.

Group Discussion

Share your reflections on Day 9 and your devotions. What does it mean to you to *surrender*? In your own experience and in your own words, share what it means to *you* to surrender to Christ. Share any areas of your life where you are excited or hopeful, or any areas where you need help, direction, or healing. If any women are considering their own path to Christ, pray for them and ask God to lead them. Find someone in the group to check in with (if possible). Come together in a closing prayer to Christ of surrender, love, and invitation.

THEME FOUR

Soul Intimacy: Your Own Relationship with God

God is boundless, transcendent, and omnipresent, touching every corner and crevice of the earth, and galaxies beyond galaxies. Yet, God is present for each and every one of us. In your own way, you have your own personal relationship with God. This relationship, this connection, will be like no one else's. Through the movements and depths of your life, heart, and soul, you speak to, receive, connect with, need, hear from, reach, call on, and know God in your own way.

Your relationship with God is truly intimate—the deepest reach of your soul coming into a profound connection with the Creator. This relationship is ongoing, never ends, and can be a constant source of overflowing love, guidance, and blessing in your life. Yours is a sacred relationship to cherish, yet also to honor, develop, and strengthen.

In the next three days, we explore the intimacy of your own relationship with God. We explore knowing God truly, in your own heart, and honoring the ways you hear God in your life. We delve into honoring your unique walk and relationship with God, one that sustains you all the days of your life.

Day 10

To Know God Personally

Then I said, "Behold I come; In the scroll of the book it is written of me. I delight to do Your will, O my God; Your Law is within my heart."

Psalm 40:7-8 NASB1995

Years ago, I came across the words of poet and playwright Ntozake Shange in her choreopoem, "For Colored Girls Who Have Considered Suicide/When the Rainbow is Enuf" and they stopped me in my tracks:

"i found god in myself
& i loved her/i loved her fiercely."

I had never truly thought about God in *myself*, and I certainly never thought about God as a *"her."* Honestly, even thinking of God as a *"her"* seemed blasphemous. Shange's words cut through this foggy layer of unawareness about the depth of my own relationship with God. One that I didn't even know could be different, deeper, and profoundly personal.

I had always thought of God as a distant, looming figure in the sky, the source of everything, indescribable yet somehow still personified as Male. I had also thought of God as removed, not actually connected to me, and certainly not within me. God existed in a realm beyond me, yet was still accessible through prayer and worship. Shange's words pierced my consciousness and traversed the depths of my experience, moving me to a place where I held and drew closer to God more deeply within my own being.

In Shange, I heard a voice that did not stand in a pulpit. I resonated with a voice that moved powerfully in her own truth and relationship with God, a voice that led me to seek that knowledge in my own life. This pushed me to go deeper, way deeper, into the very way I thought about and related to God. I wondered if how I knew and related to God flowed from my own soul or was it based on the knowledge that was relayed, given, and informed by others. I wondered how my concept of God impacted how I connected to God. And I wondered if there was more—much more—that I could be experiencing with God.

In the Bible, we see different aspects of God, different ways God is revealed and touches humanity. We see the Protector, the Provider, and the Father. We see, in the Old Testament, the judgment. Throughout the Bible, we see the intercession and revelation of God. We see the undying love as God sent Jesus Christ. In Christ, we see the eternal way of truth, compassion, and salvation. The composite of all that God is beyond all human dimensions and capacities to truly grasp in its entirety. Yet, we grasp a part of it, the part that connects with us.

As a young person, I always wanted to do the "right" thing. I connected with God as the ultimate authority, omniscient and omnipresent. My whole upbringing grew within me a hearty respect for authority, parents, leaders in school and church, and imprinted within me with clear boundaries of right and wrong. Raised in a church tradition where men held all the positions of formal leadership, I always had a sense of respect for religion. Yet, I felt a distance in how I personally connected with religion and church, leaving an unrealized gap between me and God.

Yet Shange's words challenged me: Was there actually more space for God to occupy within me? Whether I was praying for a sick relative, victims of an accident, or coming to God in heartache and tears when a beloved relationship did not end the way I hoped, I leaned into God. I leaned into prayer. I leaned hard. I needed to be close to God. To close the spaces that felt deserted, sad, and longing, that needed answers, reassurance, and hope. In those "leaning in" moments, I felt my own connection with God deepen. Me alone, one on one with God, opening my soul, with my heart wide open.

When I think of Shange's choreopoem of African-American women baring their souls, and their lives, often when marginalized, I see a connection in the longing expressed in the Psalms. In the trying times of life, we often reach up toward what is eternal and true. In Psalm 40, we see the author, David, crying out for God, seeking to be heard, needing the steadfastness of God, worshiping God with awe, and holding God in his heart:

Then I said, "Behold I come; In the scroll of the book it is written of me. I delight to do Your will, O my God; Your Law is within my heart."
Psalm 40:7-8 NASB1995

Yes, God, Your law is within my heart. My heart. The part of me that feels deeply, where I can personally cherish, honor, and love You. When I called out for God in tears and prayer, it was more than a need for rescue or help; it was a longing for a love that never fails. It was crying out for a love that would lift me, reassure me, and hold me in peace. It was reaching for a love that would sustain me through it all. It was a love I cherished. When I got up from prayer, life felt better. I felt better. I knew the sun would rise in the morning, and my soul would rise with it. Yes, I feel God in my heart, and I love God fiercely.

My experience with God, this one-on-one connection, is as vitally important as my knowledge of God, what I learn from others, and teachings about God. In my own experience, in bringing all of my soul to God, I drew closer. In speaking to God, bringing all of me and my life to God, I stepped closer. To move past the limits of what I held in my mind about who God is, allowed me to feel God profoundly in my heart. I drew close, to know, connect without limit, and relate to God as the ultimate giver of everlasting love.

As with any relationship with a friend, husband, family member, or neighbor, the more connected we feel, the more trust and the more intimacy grow. We experience a greater, deeper flourishing, receptivity, and realization of love. And, the relationship has a greater impact on you. To deepen your relationship with God, to love God and all that God is, is to open your soul to every blessed way God can possibly touch you. This opens up, guides, leads, and blesses every step of your journey. The relationship with God becomes your own compass, pointing you always toward the highest good. Truly, a personal relationship with God, like the presence of an everlasting friend to your soul, is living and breathing sustenance.

God dwells not only above, outside, and beyond us, but in the Spirit that moves the wind, the moments that stir your heart. Yes, like the Psalmist, there is a delight in doing the will of God. To feel the joy of being in sublime alignment with God's truth and with God's highest plan. To know God personally is sacred. To love God "fiercely" is to love with intention and intensity, letting nothing come between the space of you and God, letting nothing come between the connection of God in your heart. This is a mighty force to feel within. It is a sacred relationship that is yours to nurture, grow with, and unfold.

Knowing God is the most personal and profound journey. Each and every one of us has our own unique, special, and precious relationship with God. Different Scriptures, teachers, wise women, our deepest passions, and heartfelt feelings all move us and speak to us in different ways. Yet, to attune to God within your own heart, mind, and soul is to find your own blessed connection. This sacred relationship becomes a foundation to propel, support, and bless every day of your life and all that God has called you to be. You have your own way of knowing God. Honor it, love it, explore it deeply and profoundly. Let it move you, hold you, support you, and call you. Let it fill you with light and love overflowing.

Devotion

Dear God, I thank you with my whole, wide-open heart for Your love that holds me, sustains me, and that touches me every day of my life. I cherish our relationship that never ends. I am grateful to open my soul to you, to pour forth everything in my heart and mind, and come before you, God. I thank you, God, for Your boundless, everlasting love that touches and fills my heart. I pray that our relationship grows deeper and stronger every day. I pray that You strengthen every gift, talent, and blessing You have endowed in my heart to share. I thank you, God, for being with me, living within me, and loving me, every moment of my life.

Reflection

Take 10 minutes and reflect: Who do you know God to be? How would you describe the character and essence of God? How do you conceive of God? Be specific as possible.

Reflect on how you connect with God in your heart, mind, and spirit. In what ways do you personally connect with God? Describe your ideal relationship with God, one that you cherish, as vividly as possible.

How close is your relationship with God? Reflect and scan your mind, heart, and soul. Are there any gaps between you and God? How can you become even closer to God? Write down all that you hear and feel.

Write your own devotion here.

Read it quietly first and hold it deeply in your heart. Then, say it aloud in a prayer to God.

Group Discussion

Open with your devotions and reflections on Day 10. What does it mean to have your own relationship with God? How have other people or teachings shaped your concept and relationship with God? What do you know God to be, and how can you know God more personally? How would having a more intimate relationship with God impact your life? End with prayers, holding each woman in love, and blessing their own walk with God.

Day 11

To Hear How God Speaks to You

"My sheep hear My voice, and I know them, and they follow Me."

John 10:27 NASB1995

Suddenly she stops singing. On a Sunday afternoon, filled with the sound of easy blues music playing, she just stopped. And pauses. It's the scene from the movie, *The Color Purple*, when Shug, the juke joint singer, stops the show, and stops singing the song she's always sung. She takes a long pause and starts singing a new song, "Speak, Lord. Speak to Me." Then, she walks straight out of the juke joint, singing the whole way with her audience and band following behind. Shug swings open the doors to the church and sings the words directly to her preacher father and to his entire congregation, *"Maybe God is trying to tell you something, right now."*

I love this scene, the moment it captures, of the Spirit touching her, God speaking to her. I love how she heard it, paused, received it, and then acted. Throughout the Bible, we have accounts of God speaking, through signs, dreams, and revelations. The Bible forever contains this blessed wisdom, the truth, and the voice of God. Yet, as we live and breathe, there are times when our souls desperately want and need to hear from God. At many times in my life—especially at a critical crossroads, making a decision to leave something, to start something new, or embark on a path not well worn—I needed God's guidance. Yes, I can pray, plan my steps, think things through, but sometimes, like Shug, I simply call out, "God, Speak to me."

As much as I've wanted a blazing, sure-fire sign, and believe me, I have asked many times, that rarely happens. The miracles, divine intervention, parting of the Red Sea, and the burning bush, yes—I have wanted all of that. My request often has been, *"Please, God, make it plain for me to see!*

Then, one day driving home from church, I paused. I realized if every single question I brought to God was answered with a burning bush or blaze of lights, I wouldn't truly have the human experience of following, seeking, and trusting God with an open soul. Even though I love clarity, there is something precious and powerful about leaning in with faith, with full trust, and with love, to seek, know and hear from God through the often murky waters of life.

While undoubtedly, miracles, an audible voice, and unmistakable signs occur in the realm of human experience, hearing from God is often far more subtle. Hearing from God, being attuned, and listening with your body, heart, and soul, flows from *trusting God*. In as many ways we are different, there are as many ways we hear from God. We may feel it, perhaps as intuition or a sense of direction and guidance. Yet, while it may not always be clear, this is certain. Knowing that there is a loving God that touches every part of our lives, I know God speaks to us. When we come to Jesus Christ, He gives us this blessed assurance:

"My sheep hear My voice, and I know them, and they follow Me."
John 10:27 NASB1995

To come to Christ, to be with Christ, and to follow Christ, your soul rests securely in His hand. In our ongoing relationships with God, we can trust that He is with us, and you can trust and know that He indeed is speaking to you. We always have the sacred Scripture to show us the truth, His words, and to hear His voice. Yet, we still have those moments where we ask, *"Please Lord, come close, speak to me."* Perhaps God speaks through a feeling, an impression, or a vision. It could be a strong sense of knowing or a remarkable "coincidence," or an undeniable tug at your heart. In those moments, get still and listen to how God is speaking to you. Listen to the way you hear the voice of God.

There was a time when I started noticing a feeling, a nudge, and an impression to do something, usually slightly out of the context of the present moment. I would feel an impression to go upstairs right before I left the house, when I was ready to go. I would feel an impression to turn right while I was driving when my plan was to go straight ahead. At first, I would ignore or rationalize these impressions, reasoning with myself that I didn't *need* anything from upstairs, or I didn't *need* to turn right. But, inevitably, the real "reason" would be revealed: It rained later that day, and I needed that umbrella, which was upstairs! Or, I would have avoided a massive traffic backup, caused by an accident, if I had turned right!

So, I started to pay closer attention to these nudges and impressions. I started to honor them and follow where they were leading me. Over time, the nudges became more personal, more urgent, and more loving. I would get the impression to spark a conversation with a stranger. Or to hug a woman I just met and barely knew. Yet, this nudge to hug seemed quite odd, so I paid attention.

I learned to pause and listen. All of the nudges and impressions were leading me to do something good. While we all receive many sensations, feelings, mental, and emotional reactions, when we hear from God and hear His voice, it leads to the ultimate good, truth, love, and highest purpose. It leads to protection, direction, and provision. Hearing from God is to hear the nature of God. There is never an impression to strike out, to hurt, or to harm, because the nudges are always impressing the very nature of Christ upon you—urging you to express love.

I learned to listen to what the impressions were telling me. I learned to honor this sense and dwell in gratitude and receptivity to hear from God. When you truly tune in and listen, you learn to discern where it is leading. God leads us away from confusion. God fills us with peace. God leads our way with love and light. In your own peace, listen. In the sacred pause, hear and honor where God is leading you.

When you get a feeling or a knowing, there is the blessed opportunity to be still and ask God what is being revealed. In stillness, feel the connection and the guidance flowing to you. It could be a positive, negative, or even a vague feeling or a remarkably powerful sense. Ask God to help you discern, feel, and receive what He is leading you toward. In this space, listen to God:

> *Be still, and know that I am God; I will be exalted among the nations, I will be exalted in the earth!*
> *Psalm 46:10* NKJV

In your own receptive stillness, you can perceive, and know the character of God, deeply in your own mind, heart, and soul. In stillness, God may be telling you something to bless you. God may be telling you something, moving you to display His glory, for you to be a blessing to others.

When Shug flung open those church doors, she stepped forward to her father, who was preaching. He paused, and several tearful moments later, after years of estrangement, he embraced his beloved daughter and she wrapped her loving arms around him. Yet, unlike Shug, I didn't step forward to hug the woman I had just met. The nudge to hug her seemed so out of context in that moment that I rationalized it away. I reasoned that she would think my forwardness quite odd.

Instead, as I said goodbye, I let my hand rest warmly on her shoulder. Yet, even with that hand-to-shoulder contact, I thought, *"Maybe God is trying to tell me something, right now."* Maybe God was simply telling me that this woman needed to *feel love*. I made sure to honor this sense, this nudging, going forward. While it did not make sense to me at the time, I see now that it was a part of God's love moving through me.

As God speaks to us, we also speak to others. When you hear a message from a friend, pastor, a neighbor, or a passerby, that was exactly what your soul needed at the very moment—that is the Spirit moving. That is God touching you. Life gives countless decisions, opportunities, and moments to listen to God. Truly, you are a blessed portal for God's grace and love to be overflowing in your life. Simply ask, "Speak to me, Lord." And then listen.

Devotion

Dear God, I open my heart, my soul, and my ears to hear Your voice. I come before You with gratitude for the ongoing relationship we have. I thank you for Your guidance and all the ways You speak to me. I pray, God, for the wisdom, peace, and discernment to hear Your voice and Your truth above all others. I ask to be an open vessel to receive all that You impart to me. I rest in the blessed assurance that you do, indeed, speak to me, Lord. In Jesus's name, I pray, Amen.

Reflection

Pause and meditate on the opening Scripture. Repeat the words slowly. Imagine yourself hearing the voice of Christ and let it fill your heart, soul, and mind. Take 10 minutes to be in peace with God. Write down all that you heard, felt, and thought.

Consider all that is in your soul and heart right now and think of one question you have for God. Speak this in a prayer to God and allow several minutes to feel, connect, and receive. Write down all that you hear.

How do you discern wisdom, direction, and guidance from God? Have there been times where you dismissed or ignored possible guidance? Ask, and pause to listen: How can you discern guidance from God?

Write your own devotion here.

Meditate on it and hold it in your heart. Speak it aloud as a prayer to God.

Group Discussion

Start with sharing your reflections on Day 11. What does it mean to hear the voice of God? How do you know when you are hearing from God? How do you discern and process what you feel, your thoughts, hunches, and intuition? Discuss moments when you have acted or not acted on these feelings. Share your experiences and insights. End with each person sharing their Devotion. Close with a prayer lifting up each woman in her relationship with God.

Day 12

To Honor Your Walk with God

And in the morning, rising up a great while before day, he went out, and departed into a solitary place, and there prayed.

Mark 1:35 KJV

Even in the midst of being Jesus—the Son of God, God in the flesh, walking the earth, performing miracles, healing the sick, teaching, and leading his followers—even Jesus stopped and prayed. Having all the power and authority of being sent by God, Jesus practiced prayer as part of his own relationship with God. In the first chapter of Mark, we get a glimpse of the extraordinary reach and impact of Jesus. Yet, juxtaposed against the phenomenon of all that was happening, Jesus would still slip away to find solitude, to be by himself with God, and pray.

At dawn, I can only imagine Jesus in prayer, girding Himself for a new day, and hearing from God. We will never know what God said to Jesus in prayer, nor will we know what Jesus said in those private moments. Yet, what I find so remarkable, that so deeply impressed upon me: Jesus makes evident the genuine, living, and vital need to be connected with God on this journey.

In Christ, we see the intentionality in prayer. Every word He spoke was truth. Every action He took was exemplary. Christ shows us and gives us the example to follow—the importance of an ongoing practice of prayer. Like any relationship, anything of value that matters, the relationship with God is deepened with time, attention, and intention. Christ, surrounded by flocks of people that needed Him, showed us that prayer was *essential.*

Our lives can become so busy, so filled with our own pursuits, relationships, demands, and crises. Yet, your relationship with God is a constant. Through it all, every relationship, circumstance, and passing year, God is always there. And so is prayer.

Our prayer practice may be experienced in worship, in a church, kneeling beside a bed, sitting on a couch with coffee, or walking outside and staring at the predawn sky. In communing with God and in solidifying your own personal practice, you set a foundation for your life. You invest time, energy, and intention into your own walk with God. And there is a blessing, a strengthening, that flows back to you through prayer.

Every morning, when I lived in my compact Capitol Hill apartment, I would sit in my La-Z-Boy and pray. I loved the quiet personal time, where I could bring all my thoughts and issues to God. From that steady morning prayer time, I found the sustenance I needed and a vibrant, higher connection to propel me through each day. Sometimes I sought answers, and other times I simply listened. Often, I gave praise and gratitude. And God certainly heard a lot of my complaints and pleading when I was searching, seeking understanding, and figuring things out. Yet, I knew God was there, and I felt free to share everything.

Once a week, I would rise even earlier, well before dawn, and pray. On those precious mornings, I prayed to God about my 5 a.m. morning radio show. I often stayed up the night before, putting the music playlist together, creating a flow of sounds, words, and grooves to touch the soul. I would pray to God to use my voice, the music, the platform, and the airwaves for His purposes and glory. That practice became a ritual, praying to God to connect all of my journey and all of my gifts to God's greater plan.

Even though my radio hosting position was a volunteer, non-paid opportunity, it was deeply special and truly meaningful. And even though I was still figuring out my ultimate career path, freelancing and working part-time, I thanked God for all of it. I found a constant, beautiful comfort in knowing that I am with God and God is with me. That God is paving, guiding, and watching this walk. Every step, every triumph, every worry about making a living, God is with me through it all.

One morning, after signing off the air at the radio station, I went to our station mail slots and started looking through my mail. I found a handwritten envelope addressed to me and pulled out a handwritten letter. It was from an inmate at a correctional facility, where they played our station in the mornings. He heard me describe the song by Abbey Lincoln, "Caged Bird," and its connection to Maya Angelou's famous poem by the same name. His words, flowing with hope and sincerity, spoke of how he was touched to hear the song. He appreciated the message of the music, as he was reminded of his own freedom. I was so moved by his letter. It felt like a connection only God could orchestrate. In prison, tuned into a jazz radio station, he heard exactly what his soul needed. I saved that letter, and I cherished his words. I knew God was with us both.

I have come to appreciate now that the ritual of prayer, the practice of cultivating a personal relationship with God, is not just for me to be helped and guided. It is also a sustained way of honoring every step

God has given you to take. Through prayer, you honor the journey, the purpose, and the mission that God has ordained you to live.

Each of us has our own divinely appointed walk, and you honor this walk when you step into a sacred practice with God. In this relationship, you can be totally present, seen, and connected. There, you bring God everything, all of you—to touch, bless, direct, anoint, and exalt for His glorious purposes.

When I ponder the life of Christ, I treasure and marvel at the eternal wisdom, the everlasting example of honoring the walk we have with God. Yet, we know that Christ's earthly existence ended in a profoundly painful sacrifice. Jesus prayed to God, knowing of the impending crucifixion. Showing the tragic pain of his own humanity, yet still walking with God in prayer:

> *He went a little farther, and fell on the ground, and prayed that if it were possible, the hour might pass from Him. And He said, "Abba, Father, all things are possible for You. Take this cup away from Me; nevertheless, not what I will, but what You will."*
>
> *Mark 14:35-36* NJKV

Jesus, knowing what would come, still prayed to God—let Your will be done. In this prayer, Christ honors God's larger plan. The unfolding of our lives is a part of a greater plan, some parts clearly within our reach and vision, and some parts held in the greater will and vision of God. In prayer, you open your heart and lift up your soul to God. In prayer, you honor every step you take with God. And in prayer, you honor the will of God in your life—the sacred mission and purpose that God has given you.

God gives us the space to have our own unique, sustaining, life-giving relationship with Him, every step of the way. There, in your soulfully intimate connection with God, you find your center, a guiding compass in your walk with God. A quantum physicist will tell you, there is no center, no beginning or end, no middle, no top or bottom of the universe we exist in. Yet, in prayer with God, we find our sacred center—one that grounds, blesses, and propels our journey. In every step of your blessed walk with God, you have prayer. At every juncture, lift your life to the Almighty and pray—let Your will be done, and may I always honor my walk with You.

Devotion

Dear God, thank you for the everlasting, loving, and powerful truth and eternal example and blessing of Jesus Christ. Thank you for giving me a sacred relationship that I share with You. I thank you for Your presence that never leaves me. I come before You with everything, all that I am, and all that You have given me. I worship You in our moments of prayer, and I pray for Your continual guidance, every step of my life, and the journey and the calling You ordained. Thank you, God, for the profoundly blessed experience of walking with You, all the days of my life. Amen.

Reflection

Reflect for a moment on the opening Scripture. How important is your prayer life to you? What is your daily or regular practice of connecting and praying to God?

Take 5 minutes and reflect on your prayer life and personal practice of communing with God. What do you appreciate? What, if anything, is missing, and are there areas for deeper connection and exploration? How can you expand, strengthen, and deepen this practice? Write specific actions that you will commit.

Consider the power and blessing of your one-on-one relationship with God. What is most important on your walk with God now? Meditate on this. Write down all the comes to your heart and mind. Bring this now to God in a prayer.

Write your own devotion here.

Read it first silently in your heart and allow it to deeply penetrate your soul. Say it out loud as a prayer, your own conversation with God.

Group Discussion

Begin with sharing your devotions and then your reflections on Day 12. For the whole group discussion, focus on stretching the possibilities of your walk with God. Why is the practice of prayer so important? To expand our own thinking and possibilities, consider and imagine: What do you think prayer meant to Christ? How would your life calling be impacted by deepening, strengthening, or expanding your own practice of connecting with God? Share your best practices and what edifies you. End with a prayer to lift up each woman on her walk with God.

THEME FIVE

Sacred Vessel: Let Your Soul Shine

Your entire being—your heart, mind, body, and soul—is akin to a vessel. A sacred vessel through which God's purposes and glory can expand, grow, and overflow. When you devote all of your gifts, your works, and every aspect of your life to God, the light of your soul shines gloriously. Through your light, you bring light to others and the ultimate glory to God.

Being complex and beautifully human, we have numerous opportunities to become aware and intentional about our own self-development and the ultimate purposes we serve. All of the aspects of who we are affect our energy, our souls, and the light we radiate in the world.

In the next three days, we delve into strengthening the sacred vessel of who you are. We explore becoming aware of and managing the ego. We reflect on strengthening and edifying our consciousness with the Word of God. Finally, we explore the impact of committing all of your soul, your purpose, and your life to serve God. As you read and reflect, allow yourself the grace to examine and embrace all that is sacred within you, so that you may more deeply, fully, and even more gloriously let your soul shine.

Day 13

Lay Down the Mighty Ego

Let no unwholesome word proceed from your mouth, but only such a word as is good for edification according to the need of the moment, so that it will give grace to those who hear.

Ephesians 4:29 NASB1995

My mouth, my ability to express myself, is one of my biggest assets. I have always had the spark to advocate and fight the good fight. If you have a problem that needs solving, a cause that moves me, or even an unfair parking ticket, I am the woman for you! I stand up and speak out with heartfelt conviction. Yet, when my mouth fueled by ego leads the way, those moments are often less than shining.

Soon after I was baptized, I immersed myself in Bible study. I prayed to God: *Use me, all of me, my gifts, and my soul for Your glory.* Then, one evening, I had a supernatural experience, and I know this for sure, because there is no other earthly explanation.

It was the weekend, and my coworker and I were catching up, chatting at a cozy booth in a pleasant restaurant. Work was stressing me—the people, complications, and ongoing issues. Truly, I *needed* to vent. And then, I began veering into a dangerous, unproductive lane—simply complaining about other people. I became aware that my conversation was not leading anywhere good.

All that week, I had been meditating on scriptures about the power of the tongue. Yet, I continued talking, venting, and circulating negativity. I was on a roll, giving voice and energy to the very situation I claimed to not like. Then, one of the strangest things ever happened. From out of nowhere, as though I was gently touched by an unseen force, a slight pressure curled my tongue, pushed its center downward, and pulled the sides upward. This force literally raised my tongue to the roof of my mouth—which momentarily caused me to stop speaking.

I looked around as though an angel might appear and bop me on the head. I immediately knew God was getting my attention. That motion of my tongue defied physics and the capabilities of my own body. I tried to mimic the motion again, curling and raising my tongue. I could not do it then and have never been able to do it since then. Literally, in my own body, I felt God take control of the vessel—me and my ego. God grabbed hold of my attention, letting me experience a truth—all of me was to be used, *including my mouth*, for His glory.

At that moment, when I was complaining, my ego was in control. Yet, the pull, force, and direction of the Spirit are very different from the ego's draw and desires. The ego is limited and bounded by thoughts, feelings, and by what can be measured and experienced within the five senses. While the soul is unlimited, boundless, and connected to God. The ego is defined primarily by personal needs and distinction from others and often asserts itself to achieve its own desires. While the soul brings light to what truly matters, what is eternal, and serves God's grandest purposes.

On that evening at the restaurant, while it is very healthy and necessary to process challenging feelings, I went even further. I began voicing my own negative judgments, spewing and creating an atmosphere of even more negativity. Knowing it was God that touched my tongue, my ego, and pierced my awareness, made me stop and reflect on how I was using *my vessel*. I became conscious of how I used my energy and my voice—the power and potential of my vessel—to fulfill either ego-driven or spirit-led purposes. I had a real, conscious choice to make: I had to lay down my ego.

With my ego, I can destroy or uplift. I can discourage or bring light. I can weaken or strengthen and forge relationships. Yet, to lay down the ego allows the soul to take center stage, to radiate the light of God's grace. When we lay down the ego, we become more aware of how God can use the moment, our voice, energy, talents, our souls, when we attune the sacred vessel of who we are to serve a glorious purpose.

My tongue-stopping intervention gave me a moment of conscious choice—to use my words and all the potential therein—to give voice to small concerns and negativity, or to serve, create, and build the larger purposes of God. This choice did not happen immediately. Yet, through ongoing, intentional reflection and a conscious decision, our voices can be used for God's grace:

> *Let no unwholesome word proceed from your mouth, but only such a word as is good for edification according to the need of the moment, so that it will give grace to those who hear.*
> *Ephesians 4:29* NASB1995

This Scripture reminds me to be conscious of the power of the tongue. Truly, it speaks to the possibilities we hold in our own souls. We have a powerful choice to become a sacred vessel of God's grace and light. Even in the midst of a conversation, I can lay down the needs and dictates of my ego. I can lay down the need to bolster, defend against, and speak to the smallness of the moment, rather than the power of what God can do.

Yet, laying down the ego is a challenge. The ego is very much a part of who we are. I made a conscious prayer to reconcile myself to God, to yield my ego, and let Spirit lead the way. Over time, I felt the desire of my ego rise up to defend, protest and justify. I became conscious of how much energy I used to prove myself, to be recognized, and to build myself up before other people. This consciousness allowed me to observe whether I was using my voice for the highest purpose. At times, I chose to let other people's agendas, egos, and even negativity take center stage so that I could observe my own habitual, unconscious, and reactive responses. In those moments, I felt vulnerable, less bold, and less in charge. Yet, it led me to a deeper, more soulful way of using my voice.

An ego laid down feels like dropping a weapon. Without it—initially—I felt bare and exposed to injury from other people's egos. When not expressing a well-earned complaint or choosing not to return verbal fire with fire, I felt like I was crucifying my ego—binding it to a commitment to be reconciled to God. Subduing the ego, I felt the insults to my bruised ego that I chose not to defend. I felt my ego-based pride fading. With time, I began to consciously release the habitual, reactive ego expressions. I attuned to the part of my spirit that serves a greater purpose, and that requires conscious, intentional, and enlightened expression.

With a focus on God, letting His truth touch your consciousness, stir your soul, and overflow in your sacred vessel, the glorious light of your soul shines. We can consciously choose to use our gifts to serve the highest spiritual calling—peace, love, and grace—in all the moments, places, and areas we are called to be.

To lay down the ego, to surrender your soul fully to God, accomplishes the grandest purposes beyond which we could even imagine in a single moment. Our egos can envision limited areas, while God's scope is unlimited and infinite. Becoming a vessel of God, it is no longer, "Let my will be done," it is, "Let *God's* will be done." I learned, the power in my soul, the passion and conviction to speak up and stand up, is to be used for something greater. My voice was not meant to be small, pushing for my own ego, but bold, audacious, and aligned with the highest purposes of God.

We have a sacred responsibility to be stewards of ourselves—to be conscious of the power within our own sacred vessel. We can lay down the ego, the moments where we speak and act only from the ego. You can decide to open your sacred vessel to the fullest breadths of its glory—aligning your mind, voice, and gifts to the grace of God, moving you to your highest purpose. Truly, as you lay down your ego, the spirit of God overflows and shines through your blessed soul.

Devotion

Dear God, to You, I lift up all of my soul, every gift, talent, desire, moment, and every word I speak. I pray that You sanctify me and lead me in Your will. I ask for Your grace to attune all of me for Your mightiest purposes. I ask for forgiveness when I go astray and for Your power to strengthen me on the path I walk. May Your grace, love, and truth flow through my soul. I pray that all of my work, my purposes, and life brilliantly shine and glorify You. Amen.

Reflection

Take 10 minutes and reflect on the following questions: Are you aware of those moments when your ego leads, rather than your soul? When your ego is *in charge*, what personal need is being served? What greater purpose could be served if you laid down your ego? What, if anything, is preventing you from laying down your ego?

Think of an incident where your ego was leading. Now imagine the grace of God filling your voice, your mind, your talents, and your soul. What possibilities and purposes could be achieved when your soul leads and shines in that moment?

Visualize: How can your talents be used to radiate God's light? How can you strengthen your vessel to express this light? Ask God for guidance. Write down all that you feel and hear.

Write your own devotion here.

Feel it deeply in your soul and say it aloud to God as a prayer.

Group Discussion

Open with your reflections and devotions for day 13. Share freely, in a space of openness and without judgment, the ways your ego may have run the show. How can you become more aware of your ego, and what strategies can you use to manage your ego? Discuss how you can use your gifts to be a vessel of God's grace. What impact, what glory to God is possible, when you lead with your soul? End with prayers, holding up each woman, to strengthen her vessel as a glorious light of God's grace.

Day 14

Lay Your Foundation with the Word of God

"Therefore everyone who hears these words of mine and puts them into practice is like a wise man who built his house on the rock."

Matthew 7:24 NIV

A caterpillar, with its beautiful transformation, a metamorphosis from the lowly creature plodding on the ground, to the delicate butterfly floating gracefully in the air, embodies a timeless metaphor. Its process of change is very much like the human process of change we experience within, as our souls grow in the knowledge of Christ. At some point, the bodily structure of the caterpillar breaks down within itself. Then, within its cocoon, new cellular structures begin to form that support the blossoming new creature, the unfolding of its wings, and this new glorious expression of life.

In surrendering, devoting, and yielding our souls to God to become a sacred vessel of the Almighty, like the caterpillar, we, too, are completely transformed. Yet, our transformation is within. As beings of mind, soul, and consciousness, we are being transformed by the Spirit. In our change, we offer up every mindset, every belief, and every thought, to be touched, expanded, and transformed by the words of Christ. This reminds me of the Scripture, becoming a new creature in Christ:

> *Therefore if any man be in Christ, he is a new creature: old things are passed away; behold, all things are become new.*
> *2 Corinthians 5:17* KJV

Coming to Christ is a spiritual transformation from the inside out. This change begins with an intention, a desire to let all of your soul be in service to God's purpose. It involves an intention to know, study, and truly align your soul with the will of God—this grand, divine orchestration of plans and purposes, a blessed yet fully incomprehensive blueprint that is Spirit in humanity. This is a personal and sacred journey with God, where we build and strengthen ourselves from within, absorbing the power and truth of the Word of God into our being. Through prayer, communion with God, and the workings of the mystery of God, in which we are intricately and lovingly bound, a new consciousness develops.

Like the caterpillar, we experience a transformation. A new consciousness is being built, with new structures, new thinking, and new beliefs that uphold the Spirit of God flowing in our souls. But unlike the caterpillar, where the change is innate, our transformation begins with our own free will choice.

My own intentional, personal Bible study and prayer became the foundation for this personal, sacred and ongoing transformation. There were times when immersed in the reading, I could *feel* an energy, a vibrance, as though the Spirit was flowing through the words. This feeling, this presence, does not always or often happen. Yet, it shows me, as we step into a greater mystery with God, how God transforms us when we seek Him. In my study, I immersed myself in the words of Jesus and genuinely sought to understand His wisdom. I wanted to draw my soul close to His Spirit, His words, and His mission of a life sublimely attuned to God's purpose.

I felt my soul resonate deeply with His teachings, as though my consciousness was absorbing a sacred truth. Through reflective and conscious study, a new and enduring foundation was being laid in my own consciousness. This brought life and meaning to these words:

"Therefore everyone who hears these words of mine and puts them into practice is like a wise man who built his house on the rock."
Matthew 7:24 NIV

I love the metaphor within this Scripture. Like a house, we too, have a structure of consciousness, a system of beliefs that upholds and supports who we are. To put the Word of God into practice, it must dwell within us. It must live within our souls.

So my pattern became this: I would read the Bible until my mind felt refreshed, clear of any stress and confusion, until the energy of truth pierced my consciousness. I held the Bible passages up as mantras—new thought patterns—and I began to examine my existing beliefs. To do God's will, to be a sacred vessel of God's grandest purpose, I needed to absorb God's Word directly into my own thoughts and consciousness. I needed to align my inner being with the mindset to serve God.

Yet, as is often the case when building a house, excavation is required. We must examine what is present, rip out, tear down, and remove what does not sustain the new structure. As I studied and prayed, I reflected a lot on my own thoughts and beliefs, many of which I simply took for granted, as previously unexamined beliefs. I held up the Scripture as a mirror to my thoughts and beliefs. This process challenged my existing belief systems, breaking down the mental scaffolding of old beliefs, which held in place how I had defined myself up to that point. I began to see what beliefs aligned with God's Word, and importantly, what did not.

In absorbing the Word of God, I became aware of my beliefs and the unconscious foundations they were built on. I had a personal mantra, a belief, that "If it is to be, it is up to me." While my personal initiative and drive served me well, when I really began to study the Bible, I learned about the awesome power of God, which was infinitely greater than dependence on my own capacity. My underlying belief—that I had to rely solely on myself—stemmed from an unconscious belief that I could not necessarily count on others for their support. While that may be true with some people, it is certainly not true spiritually. It is absolutely not true with God.

God is omnipresent and holds power beyond what I could ever hold or conceive, giving unending support and an unfailing connection to the inexhaustible power of the Almighty. My own study led me to this truth: I must build myself, the foundation of who I am, with beliefs connected to and grounded in the truth of God. I needed new beliefs to support my unfolding consciousness—to grow, evolve, and become the woman God created and called me to be.

Deeply examining my beliefs and holding them up to the Word of God allowed me to see that my consciousness had been limited to what I could control. Those old beliefs had to go. They had to be ripped out from my old foundation to make way for the greater power of God to enter and operate within my soul, mind, and life. Like the structures break down within the caterpillar, the old beliefs broke down within me.

In laying my new foundation, I ripped up planks, floorboards, mindsets, and mentalities, and let the power, perfect truth, and grace of Scripture settle into the structure of my consciousness. As

I detached from the old thoughts, in a conscious and open space, I was reconciling my life and my soul to God's will. As we set our minds on God, the power of God becomes the spiritual authority that governs our consciousness, thoughts, and beliefs. God changes us and guides our own metamorphosis as we become new creatures.

As old thoughts, walls of the former self, and boundaries of the ego break down that do not serve the higher consciousness, you experience a transformation. Thought by thought, as new mental structures form within your being and guide your soul, you become like the butterfly, a new creature lifted by new thoughts that hold the consciousness of God's truth. You emerge, rise, and take off from a new foundation anchored in the Word of God. Shedding the old, you take flight and experience something even greater. God can shine through every facet of your being, and the purpose of the soul shines gloriously.

As I meditated on Scripture, as a personal mantra, I found a new, unshakeable strength in building my consciousness and trust in the power of God. To build, hear, and put the words of Christ into practice, we tap into an enduring, foundational strength that lies within our own souls. The words of Christ continue:

"The rain came down, the streams rose, and the winds blew and beat against that house; yet it did not fall, because it had its foundation on the rock."
Matthew 7:25 NIV

A consciousness built on the Word of God will not fall away. You establish a mighty foundation when you put the words of Christ into practice. You embody the internal fortitude to support all that God has called you to be and do. Like the butterfly, your new level of consciousness is upheld by a new foundation of thought and belief—all rooted in the Word of God. And with that foundation, you take off, radiating the light God has endowed within the sacred vessel that is you.

Devotion

Dear God, thank you for Your words that give guidance, power, and truth. I pray for Your loving direction as I learn Your wisdom and build the foundation of my soul and life. I am eternally grateful for the words of Jesus Christ. I pray to You for wisdom as I study, learn, and grow in putting the Your truth into practice. I pray that Your Word strengthens, develops, and uplifts me into becoming the woman You have called me to be. May my soul be a shining light for Your grandest, brightest, and mightiest purposes. In Jesus's name, I pray. Amen.

Reflection

Take a few minutes to reflect and scan your mind. What issue, matter, or concern is in your consciousness right now? Begin with a prayer for guidance from God, opening your mind to receive wisdom. Write down all that you hear and feel.

Imagine yourself strengthened by the Word of God in your consciousness, mind, and your decision-making. What Scripture serves as a powerful mantra that edifies you? What does it represent and mean to you?

Reflect on a major issue before you now. And now, take 5 minutes to meditate on the Scripture you chose. What insights do you feel now about the issue?

Write your own devotion here.

Meditate on it for several minutes, hold it in your consciousness, and speak it aloud to God as a prayer.

Group Discussion

Begin with your devotions and reflections on Day 14. Share one Scripture you selected as a mantra, what it means to you, and how it helps to fortify you. Share any challenges and issues where you need God's guidance. How has the Word of God given you wisdom? How does the Word of God strengthen you in fulfilling your calling? Close with prayers, lifting up the souls of each woman and strengthening her in the wisdom of God.

Day 15

Lift Your Life Purpose to Serve God

"Let your light so shine before men, that they may see your good works, and glorify your Father which is in heaven."

Matthew 5:16 KJV

Everywhere, people are searching, yearning, and needing to find purpose. Flooding the internet and social media, filling bookstores and magazines, peppering public speeches and private conversations, one essential question continually arises: *What is my life purpose?*

There seems to be something in the human psyche that propels people to search for a deeper meaning to life beyond the transactional necessities of making a living. I remember, when I was in my 20s, feeling the void of a deep, driving desire to know and to understand what my life was all about. Yet, while the specific expressions and purposes vary from person to person, I have found that in knowing and loving God, there is a simple blueprint for purpose.

What if finding and living your *life purpose* was as simple as pointing your soul to God and devoting all of your talents to the service of God? To ask, *"What is my life purpose?"* is to come before God and ask God to use all of you, every desire, ability, and vision for His purpose. Yet, this begins with knowing God and truly knowing yourself, what lies within.

In coming to Christ, I realized that my ultimate purpose was to use every God-given desire and talent for the glory of God. In this sense, purpose is not necessarily always an outcome, career, or activity. It is a *direction*. A direction within the soul, pointing and offering every gift you have to be used by God. More than being utilitarian, to be used by God is to serve a divine purpose of spiritual impact—all that God can do in and through your life. A powerful alchemy of purpose lies here. When lifting your talents, gifts, and works to serve God, others see the light in you:

"Let your light so shine before men, that they may see your good works, and glorify your Father which is in heaven."
Matthew 5:16 KJV

I love that this Scripture calls us to *shine*. Like a lamp, we radiate and glorify God. Through our being, our works, and our purposes, the energy we radiate may touch someone so deeply that they not only appreciate you, but turn to God. Truly, in pointing our works to God, there is a glory. The aftermath of what we do lies within God's mighty hand, as the impact of our works touches souls, and ripples and flows outward. This is where our purpose expands. It is not just our works, but how God uses and magnifies those works, so that others come to Christ and see the magnificent truth and purposes of God in ways we can only imagine.

I had such an encounter, feeling the impact of Spirit moving through the gifts of others while watching *Truth in Translation*, a powerfully moving play about the Truth and Reconciliation Commission in South Africa. While producing an interview with the directors and cast and helping to promote awareness of the play, I truly enjoyed hearing how this powerful work was developed. When opening night came, I was eager, and ready to sit in the audience and take it in.

The play offered a searing glimpse into truth-telling and the healing that flows from the depths of the human experience. After decades of apartheid, years of abuse, and unanswered questions for the victims of violence, in 1996, South Africa established the Truth and Reconciliation Commission. There, victims could speak their truth, and perpetrators could admit their crimes. The play, based on actual, recorded testimony of the Truth and Reconciliation Commission, allowed the audience to hear the real stories of profoundly painful human experiences.

Sitting in the audience, I could feel the rage, the pain, and even the forgiveness that flows from the soul. In one scene, a woman sang out, pleading for answers for her murdered son. Her song was filled with such depth and passion that she seemed to speak for all those who had never been spoken for. I felt the spirit of her voice emanate, as though pulsating through the depths of the oceans, covering the land, and raising the souls of victims of brutality. Her voice reverberated with a presence that filled the auditorium, honoring the souls of the victims and all those who loved them.

My soul was touched profoundly, and my tears flowed and flowed. Here was a cast of South Africans, white and black, traveling around the world with this story filled with pain and conflict. Yet, I felt hope, triumphantly so, of what the spirit of humanity and God can do. The directors used their gifts, their creativity, and their souls for a mighty purpose. The actors used their voices, from the depth of their souls, embodying pain and hate, so that a greater purpose would be served.

I left the theater deeply touched by the power of the human spirit to find healing, peace, and reconciliation in unimaginably sad, tragic realities. I felt the power and grace of the unbounded Spirit of God that makes this reality possible. A Spirit that transcends region, gender, culture, and nations—to lift souls, connect people, soften hearts, and transform reality. Truly, only the Spirit of God could move through such atrocity and pain and still move humanity toward hope, healing, and redemption.

When a soul is attuned to God, God moves through all things. The cast members, truly, had become sacred vessels, letting the Spirit of God move through their souls, bodies, voices, and works. Their blessed light poured out on the stage and filled the audience. Yet, the truth is this: I do not know the religious or spiritual orientation of any of these people. Yet, I saw their sublime devotion to their crafts, gifts, and works, and I felt the spiritual impact. I was grateful, and I witnessed what the infinite Spirit can do. Indeed, all of them beamed a radiant, shining light, letting everyone in that audience see the glory of God.

God gives us a range of varied, diverse talents and gifts—unique concentrated ways of expression and impact. Some of us may act, direct and produce plays. Others may practice accounting, design buildings, or educate youth. Yet, no matter the outlet, expression, or the works, when the power of God flows through all that you do, you become a sacred vessel for the glory of God to be multiplied. Where our works end, the power of God begins, as the impact expands beyond us and overflows.

The Spirit of God tears down walls and barriers between people, heals souls after an unimaginable tragedy, and brings forgiveness and new ways forward. When the Spirit of God breaks through, the very walls that divide us as humans crumble. The Spirit of God brings hope, changes minds, removes and loosens prejudice and hostilities. Moving without limit, the Spirit of God touches and transforms countless lives and brings their souls close to Him. Watching that powerful play in the darkened theater, I felt the brilliant glory of God shine through, unleashing the impact of people who dedicated their souls and God-given gifts to a sacred purpose. God was present, touching hearts and souls and beaming light through these sacred vessels—the actors, directors, and all the cast—in this creative play on justice and the power of human voices.

Our works—what we create and do—are within our own hands. Yet, when we lift our souls to serve God, consecrate and dedicate our works, we become part of a much, much larger purpose. Every talent, gift, relationship, desire, and vision you have—can be used for God's purpose. This direction of pointing all of you and everything toward God becomes, in and of itself, a powerful life purpose. Your life purpose now becomes to let your light shine in all God has endowed in you.

When serving God becomes the guiding force for your life purpose, there is no limit to your light and no limit to God working through your light. As you do your work, knowingly and unknowingly, other people will see, feel, and be transformed by your light. Through you, others may grow closer to and glorify God. As they come to know the power and love of the Spirit of God, they may move into their own sacred relationship with God.

We have no idea how God's grace or glory works. Yet, we must do the work, share the love, and shine the light God has given us. As a sacred vessel, when you follow God with all of your soul, you step into expansive and uncharted territory. Your gifts and talents serve a higher purpose, bringing love, compassion, connection, and peace. Truly, when you lift your soul to God, you light up our world. Let all of you, your works, your purpose, and your passions, be lifted toward God, and may your light radiantly illuminate the woman God has called you to be.

Devotion

Dear God, I thank You for every gift, desire, and talent You have placed in my soul. I pray that You touch all of me, every aspect of my life, and anoint my works for Your purposes. May Your love radiate in my soul, as I fulfill the purposes and life You have called me to live. I pray that Your will, will be done, as I commit all of my works to You. I pray to be filled with Your light as I commit to being a sacred vessel of Your most glorious light and grandest purposes. With profound gratitude, I thank You, God. Amen.

Reflection

Take a few minutes to reflect on your *life purpose*. How important is the fulfillment of purpose in your life? Whether you are certain of your purpose or searching to understand, consider how letting God use every aspect of you can fulfill your grandest purpose. Write down all that comes up.

Reflect for a few moments on a key area of your life where you devote significant time and energy. Now imagine lifting this area up to God. Ask God for guidance on how you can let your light shine even brighter.

Consider any area of your life that you feel is *not* serving God. Write down all that comes up. Now imagine how God could use this area. How can your light shine in this area? Ask God for direction and write down all that you receive.

Write your own devotion here.

Hold it deeply in your soul, feel it within, and say it aloud in a prayer.

Group Discussion

Open with your devotions and reflections on Day 15. Share your thoughts about what "life purpose" means to you? Do you feel that serving God with your whole soul fulfills your purpose? Discuss your own awareness of your "light." What does it mean to you to "Let your light shine"? Imagine the depth and breadth of what God can do with each woman in the group. How does it impact your life purpose to know that God can work through you? End with prayers, lifting up the soul, light, and purpose of each woman to God.

THEME SIX

Blessed Connection: The Power of Trusting God

Trust is everything, in all things, connecting all of us, and all of our lives, to God. Trust flows in faith, in surrender to God's will, His providence, and the Almighty hand that touches every aspect of His blessed creation. We, too, are a sacred part of that creation. While we may have glimpses, a sense, or even a soul-deep knowing of God, we can neither see nor touch as a beloved human being. Yet, we can know God, connect with, and trust God deeply in our souls.

In the gap between our actual lives, filled with joys and trials, and the soul's deep longing for God, trust fills in the empty spaces and the ongoing mysteries. Trust is a journey of deepening your relationship with God, your own blessed connection that sustains, inspires, and guides your life. As you reflect deeply and appreciatively on your own experiences and lean in with your soul, even more completely to God, trust grows. In these next three days, trust leads the way. Trust that God is at the center and the pinnacle of it all. Trust in your sacred walk with God. Trust in the unending power of your blessed connection with God that sustains and empowers you every day of your life.

Day 16

To Trust in God Almighty above All

To You, O Lord, I lift up my soul. O my God, in You I trust.
Psalms 25:1-2 NASB1995

The stoplight was red, so I called a friend. No answer. Anxiously, I pushed the talk button on my steering wheel and called another friend, a man whom I once dated. Again, no answer. Then, I started crying. Louder and louder, heavier and heavier, until I was praying, pleading, and screaming at God. Drained, exhausted, and emotionally depleted, I desperately needed someone to lean on, someone to comfort me. I cried out to God, "Why is no one here for me?

I had a long day, checking my 92-year-old grandmother, with an excruciatingly painful case of shingles, into a nursing home. Every time the sensations shot through her body, reverberating in waves of pain all over, she grabbed her head and cried out. Witnessing her suffering, I could do nothing. I could only be with her ensure she received the best possible care and that she was as comfortable as possible for the night. Now, sitting in the parking lot of IHOP, I gripped the steering wheel of my car, crying and screaming. I let it all out. Then, I took a deep breath and just sat for a while. Screaming at God, I realized, was not going to change anything. I was exhausted and hungry.

Sitting down at the booth, flipping through the familiar laminated menu, I called my mom. Still talking through tears, I recounted all the details of my tiring and difficult day. The restaurant was almost empty, except for a family sitting across the aisle and a man dining at the booth in front of me with a friend. Finally, my food arrived, and I started feeling a little better. Pancakes at night do have a soothing effect! Then, as the man in front of me stood up to leave, he turned to me and asked if I would mind if he bought my meal. I cheered up and told him, yes, thank you! I would really appreciate it. I had a *rough* day. He replied with calm comfort, I know. I heard. Immediately, I felt an answer to my prayer.

Driving home, I felt calm and at peace. Then, piercing the quiet, I heard a voice. It felt like it was outside of me. Yet, the voice came clearly into and penetrated my awareness and said, *"I am your provision."* I heard the words. I felt them in my soul undeniably. God had heard my cries. While I was wailing, crying, and searching for someone to fill the sadness, God answered. God sent a kind soul with a sensitive heart and a caring spirit to comfort me. God sent, with His unmistakable message to me, the deep comfort my soul needed—to know without a doubt that God is with me at all times.

Yet, while God's words that evening, *"I am your provision,"* gave me assurance, they ushered me into an even greater journey in trust. While I know God is real and present, I honestly asked myself, do I fully trust God in *all* things? I pray to God, I seek God ... but do I *trust* God completely? Do I trust God's truth and promises, without question, without doubt, or hesitation? There were places in my life, in my soul, where my trust in God was solid. When it came to praying for my grandmother, I lifted her up, determined in my soul that she would be fully healed. I prayed passionately, with resolve, that God would bring her through every step. And He did. Gratefully, she emerged from the nursing home, well and at peace. Yet, to trust God completely means yielding to something greater, something that extends far beyond what we can control, know, rely on, and understand. In my weakness, in areas of my life where things were not going as I wanted, I realized, perhaps, I didn't truly *trust* God in *all* things at *all* times.

The night of my breakdown at the IHOP, the "friend" I called was a man I dated in whom I once had high hopes. When the relationship ended, we transitioned to being friends. Yet, the breakup left me with a gap. A gap in my life of the deep intimacy that I wanted to share, of the comfort of someone who would always be there for me, through everything, that I could lean on and trust completely.

Reflecting on my prayers, I realized that when I prayed to God about this desire, I didn't trust—I *bargained*. I prayed to God: I need someone, just one person to lean on, *then* I can continue and fully devote all my gifts, my life, to Your purposes. At the time, I felt that serving God, which is of utmost importance to me, meant personal sacrifice, serving others, and therefore not necessarily about personal fulfillment. So, I bargained, asking for something in exchange to fill in the empty, hurting place while I navigated life. While my desire was pure and intentioned with love, that "bargaining prayer" was not truly a prayer. My words communicated distrust and conveyed my own hesitation about completely trusting God on my path.

Maybe in the long spaces of waiting, anticipating, building up a promising love connection, having it fall away, and then rising again hoping to meet a new love, I didn't fully trust that God would provide what I desired. I acknowledged and examined this honestly. Bringing it all before God, and asking God to touch all of me, even that which I don't understand, is to open up in trust—a trust that is total and complete. To trust is to know and believe in the nature of

God—what I feel in my spirit and the truths revealed in Scripture. To trust God is to know that God guides, leads, moves, and is present always—even in those places where it is dark, lonely, and confusing. Even there, especially there, to trust God is to know that God is, indeed, with you.

Trusting God, I lift all my desires, thoughts, needs, hopes, visions, and even my fears to the providence of God. Truly, trust becomes a powerful orientation of your being, where you hold God at the center of your mind and trust, with every aspect of your life, the power and truth of God above all.

Yet, while God's words—*"I am your provision"*—stayed with me, changed me, and deepened my trust, there was still more work to do. Several years later, I met a man with whom I shared synergy, an easy rapport, warmth, and friendship. Yet, after building slowly, talking for hours upon hours, and spending time together, what I thought was growing into a special relationship did not turn out the way I hoped. I was utterly confused and hurt. My mind kept processing it, over and over, trying to make sense of what happened. Then, in a pause that interrupted the flow of my thoughts, a question came clearly into my mind. I heard God ask, *"Do you trust me?"* And, even while hurt and deeply disappointed, I answered, "Yes, God. I trust You."

To you, O LORD, I lift up my soul. O my God, in you I trust.
Psalms 25:1-2 NASB1995

God had been speaking to me on this journey of trust for years, and I had to live the experience of trusting God completely. This question, *"Do you trust me?"* pointed me to a barrier to fully trusting God that I needed to remove. I had to confront in my own consciousness anything and anyone, including this search for a man, that I put on a pedestal higher than God. I had to take down and cast aside any beliefs or disbeliefs, needs or mindsets, desires or fears that blocked any part of me from completely trusting in God, His providence, and His provision. Even though I was saddened, I felt a deep trust and a deep knowing within—with God, *all is well.* I placed God on the throne of my mind to reign in every moment. For all that is, all that is unfolding, and all that will be—I will trust in God.

This journey unveiled a powerful lesson—that trust in God develops, deepens, and grows stronger as you live your life, learn, love, and grow. Trust is a process of going deeper, yielding more and more of the territory of yourself, of your heart, soul, mind, and life, to knowing God. When you fully trust God, you enter into a journey that is uniquely and powerfully yours, touching every aspect of who you are. Your trust in God becomes your own sacred, blessed connection, boundless and overflowing with the grace of God that speaks to you, comforts you, and is with you, always.

Devotion

Dear God, to You, I lift up my heart, my soul, my mind, and every aspect of who I am. I lift up all that I hope, envision, and desire to Your providence and Your provision. Completely, I trust in You, God, and am filled with gratitude for Your sacred connection with me. I am grateful for all that You have created me to be, called me to do, and the path I walk with You. To You, O Lord, I lift up every aspect of my life. In all times, in all things, and in all places, dear God, I trust in You. Amen.

Reflection

Take a few minutes and deeply reflect on trust. What does it mean to you to trust God? How do you define trust? Write down all that you feel and know.

Are there any areas in your life where trusting God has been a challenge or that you would like to strengthen? Contemplate for a moment: Are there any blocks or issues that impede this trust?

Imagine the full power of trusting God without limit, in all times, places, and things, and in every matter in your life and world. Take 10 minutes to meditate on this. What does the full power of trust in God mean for you and your life?

Write your own devotion here.

Feel trust deeply in your mind, heart, and soul, and lift your words to God.

Group Discussion

Open with your devotions and reflections on Day 16. Share your thoughts about what trust in God means to you. How does trust in God operate in your life? Share any areas where you would like to grow in or strengthen trust. How can you deepen trust? For each woman, consider: How does trusting God impact who you are, your purpose, and your calling? As a group, how can we offer support or insight to each other on this trust journey? Close with prayer, lifting everything discussed and every woman up to God.

Day 17

To Honor the Path where God Leads You

Our steps are made firm by the Lord, when he delights in our way; though we stumble, we shall not fall headlong, for the Lord holds us by the hand.

Psalms 37: 23-24 NRSV

Greatness is built step by step, one decision at a time. There is a process to success. Take one step at a time, especially the most challenging ones, and do not lose sight of the vision. *Keep going.* I have gathered these mantras over the years, listening to successful entrepreneurs and business leaders who started small with a powerful idea, then led with guts, passion, and resolve to realize their visions. Yet, before they were highly profitable and widely known, they knew themselves, and they knew where they were going.

In business, there is a clear, tangible outcome: a profitable, productive, and impactful enterprise. The path to success, as commonly presented in our culture, is a series of upwardly mobile steps, one step leading to the next, with clearly delineated markers of professional advancement along the way. Yet, in our personal lives, there is not always a clear path. While it is possible to take control of your life and align every action to achieve your goals, certain steps lie beyond our control. Things happen to our loved ones; an unexpected tragedy, a debilitating injury, or a sudden loss can change everything. We may find ourselves dealing with a reality we did not choose. We may be in moments of a glorious, sweet zone where life is humming harmoniously. Or we may find ourselves in a place where the path is not clear at all, figuring it out and waiting.

As author Alicia Britt Chole describes in her book, *Anonymous: Jesus' Hidden Years ... and Yours,* God gives us periods of waiting and developing along our own path, where our steps and actions might not always feel like a clear roadmap to success. Watching Chole on a TBN television special, she asked us to consider the developments in Jesus's life, his first 30 years, before the three years of his public ministry, a period of time during which little is known or recorded. In each year, in this "anonymous" period, with every step Jesus was taking, he was growing and preparing for the work He would do for all humanity as the Lord, Jesus Christ. Chole invites us to consider and examine our own "anonymous" periods—places of personal preparation and development—and how the growth and meaning we find at each step propels our journeys.

Life unfolds within and between our steps. In times of waiting and preparation, the steps can seem slower. Often, this kind of preparation is not formal. It unfolds organically, almost imperceptibly in moments throughout life—where you grow in your own character and learn who you truly are. These are the moments when you learn to trust in God through all the steps life takes you. At some steps along the path, there may be wonderful successes to extract insight and wisdom. At some junctures, we forge blessed connections with people we touch and who touch us. Yet, at some steps, the setbacks and detours are the very places you develop the deepest capacity of your soul to trust in God.

In this place, and through all of life, we can benefit from contemplating God's magnificent view of our life. Imagine this amazing, interconnected web of life, people, and circumstances, with the hand and Spirit of God underlying and guiding it all—every single step we take. To look at our steps, each and every one, and imagine how might God view our turns, dips, and our climbs. I cannot even fathom a scintilla of what God orchestrates. Yet, trusting God, knowing God is present, with us and for us at all times, in all places, in all things, there is meaning in every step.

Our steps are made firm by the Lord, when he delights in our way; though we stumble, we shall not fall headlong, for the Lord holds us by the hand.
Psalms 37: 23-24 NRSV

When I step back and contemplate the grandest possible view of my life, I see that my journey has been made up of many steps and decisions along the way. Some decisions I love, some I wonder why I ever made them, and some have seemingly led to nowhere. Yet, trust in God closes the gaps between what we know and what we cannot know—what is unfolding in our sacred journey. So, when I embrace the belief that there is a grander purpose in all of life, that God holds us by the hand and is with us through it all, I lean in to find the deeper spiritual meaning in every experience.

This Scripture gives us blessed assurance that God leads us on our paths. In the midst of our moments, we find a deeper unfolding of our own connection with God. We lean in to receive God's wisdom and to appreciate the significance, the blessing, and the divine purpose, of each and every step and how each step prepares us to fulfill the purposes God has endowed in our lives. This deepens our spiritual awareness and the power of trust—as we know that we are, indeed, walking with God.

Knowing God's hand touches every fiber of my life, I learned to honor the entire process, each and every step—*all* of it. I learned to honor the patchwork, the divine purpose of life, being sewn together. While I may stumble, there will be no falling "headlong," as there is meaning in rising again and taking the next step. At times, when life does not unfold perfectly or ideally, I may be tempted to judge myself and my life. Yet, trusting God and knowing that His hand undergirds our becoming, we find wisdom in our own experiences. We find power in our steps and purpose in walking our paths.

Gratitude, along the way, deepens trust and allows you to appreciate the journey. Whether you are in the midst of a tremendous success or in the depths of abject pain, say *thank you* to God, not necessarily for the experience, but for the connection with Him that endures. This expression of gratitude steadies the mind and elevates you to a place to find wisdom, grace, and vision. With gratitude, you can meet every moment—good or bad, pleasurable or painful—with the powerful perspective that comes from trust in God. Each step of the journey is an opportunity to invite God to come into every choice, every relationship, and each and every fork in the road. Here, you will find strength in your own steps and a more powerful connection to the path God leads you.

With trust in God—believing in the truth of God at all times—we can take firm, certain steps and take them with confidence. As the Almighty hand of God always guides, I learned to honor what God has endowed in my heart, soul, and path—the purposes, experiences, and blessings that flow in and through my life. When we honor our walk with God, we see that every roadblock, challenge, and triumph is part of the preparation and path. Truly, to behold your every step of life, as beautifully and powerfully as God holds you, is to embrace the woman God has called you to be.

God the Almighty leads your life—your purpose and your calling—step by powerful step. With your every vision, hope and dream, honor and trust God. Surrender to His plan and providence as you live and fulfill your part in His glorious plan. Step by step, as you walk your sacred path, know that God is with you every single step of the way.

Devotion

Dear God, I dwell in gratitude and blessed assurance for Your Almighty Hand that is with me every step of the way. I rest, fall, sit, stand, and pray in the blessing of Your presence in every moment of my life. With my soul lifted to You, I trust in You, God. I honor the path You lead and the purposes You have anointed and prepared for me. I pray for Your grace all the days of my life as I walk in the power of Your glory, on my path as the woman You have called me to be. With endless gratitude, I thank you, God. Amen.

Reflection

Imagine God holding you through every step of your life. Now consider, what does it mean to honor the path God leads you on? Write down all that comes to your mind.

Imagine taking a bird's-eye view of your life. Envision your most successful or most challenging moment. What did you learn about yourself and your connection with God in those moments?

Envision yourself with a direct beam of light, connecting you to God in the midst of today's world, to where you stand now. Take a few minutes to deeply feel and contemplate this. How does your trust in God guide and empower the steps you take in life?

Write your own devotion here.

Say your devotion out loud to God in a prayer.

Group Discussion

Open with your devotions and reflections on Day 17. What does it mean to you to walk with God? Share specific examples. What does it mean to trust in God during uncertainty or difficult times? What does it mean to trust in God during blessings, joys, and triumphs? Consider how your connection with God is strengthened by trusting in Him at all times. How does your trust in God make firm the path you are on? Close with prayer, embracing every woman, in every moment, in all her steps.

Day 18

To Find Courage through Trust

I hereby command you: Be strong and courageous; do not be frightened or dismayed, for the Lord your God is with you wherever you go.

Joshua 1:9 NRSV

We were feeling wonderful, filled with the deeply satisfying joy that flows from a job well done. It was our second day of the mission trip in Kenya, and we had just finished a full day of serving, learning, and connecting. I felt lifted up by the spirits of the students we met and the commitment and love of the staff and school leaders. Headed back to our hotel in Nairobi, I was enjoying the view from the van, dust flying up, gazing at the scenery, the colorful storefronts, the occasional donkey, and the mopeds whizzing by. I was looking forward to relaxing and having dinner with the team. Finally, after about a two-hour drive, the van pulled into our hotel parking lot. Instead of being met with the comfort of being "home," we were confronted with news that changed everything. Less than a few miles away, a fire was raging at Westgate Mall in Nairobi. It appeared to be a terrorist attack.

Before we left for Kenya, our mission team laid all the plans for what we would do. The lead pastor led us in lessons, spiritual messages from the Bible at our team meetings. We learned the basics of the health care protocols for the temporary medical clinic where we would be serving on the intake team, checking patients in, and taking their blood pressure. I delved into my own serious preparation—reading the Bible, packing everything I could think of, and setting my mindset to be focused for the mission. I came to Kenya ready ... but not for this. Now, I could only trust in God.

Sitting with the team in the hotel lobby, as we watched the news in disbelief, the horrifying picture became clear. Terrorists had seized the mall in the middle of a pleasant afternoon as people were shopping, eating, and enjoying life with family and friends. Several children had even been showing off their culinary skills in a children's cooking competition. The gunmen unleashed a rampage, ravaging the joyful calm of that day, shooting indiscriminately, throwing grenades, igniting fires, and holding people hostage. In the newscasts, even the news anchors prayed and called on God. Fervently, I prayed to God, *Please help!* I called on God to help the police end this, save those held captive, and please deliver them safely. I prayed for the souls and the loved ones of those whose lives were lost and prayed for the safety of all nearby. I prayed this would end. And I prayed, *God, please be with us.*

After much consideration and prayer, we decided to continue with our mission to distribute the massive amounts of food and get the medical clinic up and running at the church. Yet, for me, aware that the siege was still raging on, I felt an underlying, nervous unease. Riding in our van, we could see and smell the smoke rising from the fires the terrorists set at the Westgate Mall. It was frightening to think of what was still happening there and what could happen to anyone in the city. At that moment, I *needed* church like I never have before. I needed comfort and blessed assurance. I needed to hear from and be with people who believe in God and believe that God is with us. I needed that inpouring of faith. I needed to feel love in the midst of tragedy. Truly, I needed to feel God amongst us.

That Sunday, we went to church while terrorists still held innocent lives hostage. Holding hands with the congregation of the World Hope Church, we prayed to God. Praying to God before this mission, I had no idea how our purposefully laid plans would change. We came to serve, and we did. But now, I felt like an even greater experience of trusting God—something we would learn in the midst of this moment—was ultimately a major purpose of this mission.

As the city and the police were on the highest alert, checking vehicles at traffic stops throughout the city and guarding building entrances with high-powered weapons, there was nothing in my hand or in my control except prayer. As danger and uncertainty surrounded us, I felt what it means to totally trust and lean on God.

> *I hereby command you: Be strong and courageous; do not be frightened or dismayed, for the Lord your God is with you wherever you go.*
> *Joshua 1:9* NRSV

This Scripture, words of deliverance and power, is part of God's charge to Joshua to deliver his people. We, too, needed deliverance. I prayed to God, who is sovereign, to be with each and every one of us, to be in the midst of that mall, and to deliver everyone. In the midst of fearful circumstances, the Scripture gives us the command to not let fear overtake us and to know that God is bigger than every fear and any circumstance. We are assured that God is with us wherever we go and bigger than any tragedy or travesty humans can mercilessly lay on each other. We have a powerful command: to be strong and courageous in the mission God has given. Truly, to lay hold of the command, God's word of power and truth fortifies the soul with courage that flows from trust in the Almighty.

That Sunday, I felt strengthened. And, in a state of profound and absolute trust, I felt the seeds of courage growing in my spirit. We came together and prayed as a community of faith with full trust in God, to not believe that terror will win, but that the Spirit of God and the people of God will triumph. God felt so real and so present while I was holding hands in prayer with people who love Christ and trust that God is the way. I leaned into the power of trust—trust that the God Almighty who brought us to Kenya would fuel us through every challenge as we persevered in doing good works, which give the glory to God.

Looking at the sun in the bright sky over Nairobi, Kenya, I was comforted to know that the same God I pray to thousands of miles away, in the comfort of my home in the United States, was there amongst and with us all. I felt how trust, overflowing in the soul, becomes courage. In trusting God, we find our own power—the fortitude, the energy, the heart, and the will—to go as God has commanded. Here, our trust becomes personal. As you lean into trusting God so completely, it becomes a part of you—a feeling, a knowing, a certitude that you possess. And this trust also changes you.

As you embody and embrace trust, states of fear transform into courage. As you walk in the power of trust, you deepen your inner knowing that—whatever your mission, purpose, or calling—with God, it will be done.

God commands us to be courageous, to be bold, and to face what lies ahead. God imparts us to stand strong. It is our sacred choice to receive His impartation. When you reflect on all that you have accomplished and all you have yet to accomplish, trust in God. Trust supplies you with the overflowing courage to meet the mission God has outstretched before you. Your trust in God equips you to fulfill every purpose the Almighty has placed in your soul.

Devotion

Dear God, to You, O Lord, I lift up my soul to be strengthened by Your power, Your word, and Your truth. I thank you, God, for the mission, purpose, and the calling You have given me. In my walk with You, I will be courageous. I will not be dismayed. I will not yield to fear or circumstance. I will call on You, and I pray that You will strengthen me and fill me with courage, this day and every day. Thank you, God, for our blessed connection that uplifts me, and holds me, and always endures. Amen.

Reflection

Take 10 minutes to reflect on the scripture for Day 18 and the command to "be courageous." When you think of courage within yourself, what comes to mind?

Reflect on what is most salient in your life now. How could deepening your trust in God impact your life? How could strengthening your courage enhance your life mission?

Courage is a command from God, yet it must also be experienced and developed. Think of a time in your life when you were courageous. What were you believing that made your courage possible? How can you build on and further develop your courage?

Write your own devotion here.

Hold it powerfully in your heart and say your devotion out loud to God in a prayer.

Group Discussion

Open with your devotions and reflections on Day 18. Share your personal experiences of courage, times when you were courageous, and what you were believing, feeling, and thinking. How did you think of God in those moments? How did you define yourself in those moments? How can you build on that courage and deepen it? For each woman, consider and share how courage enables you to accomplish your personal mission. Close with prayers of courage and strength, lifting up each woman to God as she fulfills the mission God has endowed in her soul.

THEME SEVEN

Sacred Summoning: The Power of Your Calling

In the search for meaning, purpose, and mission in life, the idea of being "called" by God provides certainty, clarity, a definitive knowing of your direction from God, and your connection to all of life. For many, this search for one's calling can be an elusive, winding, and frustrating road. While for others, the calling is clear, tangible, and compelling. A calling is like a beautiful song, so arresting that when you hear it, it stops you, and moves you deeply—you know it is yours.

With deep certainty deep in my own soul, I know we are all "called" by God. While it may be experienced and expressed differently, the calling is your own sacred summoning in life—what moves you, touches you, compels you, and inspires you—to respond with your soul. In your response, aligned with your deepest spiritual connection to God, your actions—what you feel, do, build, create, lead, love, and express—bring the light of God through you and to our world.

In the next three days, we explore this sacred summoning, what moves your soul to respond, the purpose in your calling, and the power of your calling when it becomes a blessed, sacred, and overflowing way of life.

Day 19

The Compass of Conviction

For I am convinced that neither death, nor life, nor angels, nor rulers, nor things present, nor things to come, nor powers, nor height, nor depth, nor anything else in all creation, will be able to separate us from the love of God in Christ Jesus our Lord.

Romans 8:38-39 NRSV

It just felt wrong, on the inside, like something searing inside of me. And even though the pastor talked to millions of people, through television and radio broadcasts, and I can only imagine the countless people led to Christ as a result, hearing that message, hearing him talk decisively about the "role" of women as if he could ultimately dictate the penultimate purpose for every woman, just felt wrong. And it was. It was simply not true.

This clarity I found about truth and purpose, that I feel and know now, did not come easy. I had to listen very closely to what I was feeling. I had to *hear* this searing in my soul, and I had to bring all of it to God. When I first came to church, I had this refreshing, wide-open feeling that with the love of Christ, all things are possible. Now, I was learning new teachings, hearing preaching at women about their specific "roles," which felt limiting and constricting to my soul. A real discord churned within me.

I had to sort through the layers of authority, of the people standing in pulpits—surely well-meaning and well-intentioned—who were interpreting Scripture to tell me what God really intends for women. And to tell me, who I, as a woman, was supposed to be. Their words conflicted with a deeply-rooted, gut-level truth I felt within. I started to read the Bible and ask, *What does this mean?* I found a connection with the passages. More than words and a religion that exists as a set of rules outside of me, I found a deep connection within my soul and with God. I brought everything to God—all my questions, all my feelings, and all my discord. I had to trust what was stirring my soul.

Before I joined the church, I found truth in the fire of feminism: a deep certainty rooted within me that all of God's creation has a voice, including women, in all times, in all places, and in all things. Now, as a baptized Christian, fully committed to God, I wondered if my "feminism" was roaring up, propping up my ego, and possibly standing in the way of a full surrender to God. Surely, I did not want to be on the wrong side of sin. I asked myself—*who am I to forge my own Christian path?* Or was I placing the thoughts of others, informed as they may be, above my own, letting fear and doubt overtake my own trust in God? My soul was stirring, and God was beckoning me to listen.

Absolutely no part of me has ever believed that any belief system, including interpretations of religion, should ever deny the full personhood or agency of any human being—including the purpose, possibilities, and calling of a woman's life. All people are created in the image and likeness of God, and the connection of each person to God is a profound blessing. This lens of gender, coupled with religion, that prescribed roles or limits to women on what is possible with God did not agree with my soul. This lens did not allow for the deep understanding of the vast possibilities within any woman's soul, which contains a multitude of gifts and blessings. Her soul, her voice, her life, and her calling are hers—to feel, know, steward, and fully bring into alignment with God.

The discord that I had been feeling was more than a disagreement. It was a conviction, deep in my conscience, an unshakable knowing. My strongly felt conviction propelled me to ask God, *What is true here? What is needed here? What honors You?* This conviction arose and stood in my soul—an unshakeable belief in the calling that God has given *all* people. God plants something sacred in our souls that must be manifest through our lives. This conviction was not to be pushed aside, but honored, as the stirring within my soul was as strong and clear as the love of Christ. Indeed, as strongly as my soul was convicted, I held on even stronger to Jesus Christ.

> *For I am convinced that neither death, nor life, nor angels, nor rulers, nor things present, nor things to come, nor powers, nor height, nor depth, nor anything else in all creation, will be able to separate us from the love of God in Christ Jesus our Lord.*
> *Romans 8:38-39 NRSV*

This Scripture has always moved me—its words the fiercest, most determined belief that nothing on this planet will separate me from Christ. The words stir my soul, carrying an energy so seared to Christ, to allow no space between you and God. Conviction pulls every part of your soul into an unfailing bond with Christ. Truly, to be bound with Christ is like a divine compass that gives powerful direction for navigating all things. This compass points us to God and points us to what is sacred as we respond to life, use our gifts, and answer the call of God. This compass also serves as a check—to examine what moves you, stirs you, and to explore the questions, the ethical and personal challenges that arise in life. With your compass, you ask yourself: *Is this conviction in alignment with the love and truth of Jesus*

Christ? Truly, a woman filled with the fire of what God has given her need not be bound. Rather, she dwells in the mighty and infinite possibilities of what the love of Christ can do.

I have long admired black women spiritual leaders who have drawn on their faith, followed their calling, and infused the grace of God into the very midst of oppression. These women did not fit into artificial limitations, dictates, or prescribed expectations of what women should ultimately be. Not at all. They followed their convictions, and the words they spoke influenced and inspired generations. Strong women, like Harriet Tubman, had an enduring and lifelong connection to God that elevated and propelled them past the boundaries of enslavement, oppression, and opposition. Tubman, along with many others who have gone unrecognized in the larger pages of history, could not have blazed bright new paths—leaving freedom, peace, love, and the glory of God in their wake—unless God was with them. The God-ordained conviction of many women, who followed the calling of their souls, was crucial to the elevation of humanity. They *listened* to this calling, yielding overflowing blessings to all of God's people.

To trust your own conviction, to listen to what your soul resonates to as you connect deeply with God, lights both your purpose and your path. When we listen to the summoning in our souls, we bring God's light and grace to the world through our lives. The discord I felt, as I listened to the pastor's words, was my own soulful conviction, stirring, churning, and moving me to speak out loud what God gave me to share. It was a conviction to speak expansively, without limit and in all spaces, about the vast possibilities, power, and impact of each and every woman when she honors the calling of God in her own soul.

When your soul answers with a deep resounding *"Yes"* to what God has given you to be and do, that is, by definition, extraordinary. Your calling, uniquely yours, is divinely given. Whether your calling is lovingly supported or strongly challenged by others, it belongs to you and God. It is yours to honor and to act upon. Our callings magnify God's love in our world. Our callings often transcend, break through, shift, and change what previously has been accepted as normal and commonplace. Our callings bring forth the unique purposes, what must be birthed in our lives, that flow from our own sacred conviction.

By following the compass of your soulful conviction, you fulfill a purposeful part in God's plan—the ever-unfolding, glorious experience of humanity. Every person hears and receives their calling and conviction differently. To some, it may feel like a relentless drive. To others, a soothing feeling or a drumbeat within summons you. Still, others may hear a rising call, a loving urge, or an unmistakable knowing of exactly what must be done. This summoning has no limits, as it points you to God Almighty. When you honor your conviction, you answer your sacred call—the full impact of a woman's soul unleashed by an almighty God. When you honor God, holding fast to the love of Christ, the glory of God overflows through you, through everything and everywhere the Almighty God has called you.

Devotion

Dear God, I thank you for all that You have called me to do. I thank you for the stirring in my soul, what moves my heart, and the conviction to follow You completely with every ounce of my soul. I pray that my love of Christ will always be a mighty, clear, and unfailing compass that guides me in every step You have given me to take. I cherish the gifts, purpose, mission, and calling You have given me as sacred. I will follow You always, lift my soul to You, and I pray the blessings will be overflowing in all You have called me to be and do. In Jesus's name, I pray. Amen.

Reflection

Reflect for a few minutes on "conviction." Let it settle into your heart and soul. What does conviction mean to you? How can conviction bring you closer to God? Write all you feel and specific experiences.

What does it mean to have an impenetrable bond between you and Christ? Scan your life and heart. How can growing even closer to Christ impact your life now?

Reflect for a few minutes on your "calling," whether you are firmly in the midst of it, at the beginning, or in the process. Reflect on the Scripture for Day 19. How can your love of Christ guide, inform, and shape your calling?

Write your own devotion here.

Hold it deeply in your soul and say your devotion out loud to God in a prayer.

Group Discussion

Open with your devotions and reflections on Day 19. Share your personal experiences of conviction: What were you feeling within? What was moving you? How did you respond? Consider and discuss the ways God speaks to us through our souls. Share personal examples or stories from the Bible. How can focusing on Christ and praying to God align your conviction with God's will? For each woman, consider and share how honoring your "conviction" connects you more deeply with your calling. Close with prayers, lifting each woman's soul up to God as she honors the calling God has given her.

Day 20

The Crown of Purpose

For we are His workmanship, created in Christ Jesus for good works, which God prepared beforehand so that we would walk in them.

Ephesians 2:10 NASB1995

It was a normal Monday morning. I sat down at my desk and started to pull out my agenda for the week. Before I could take a sip of my coffee, the office manager walked over and asked, "Why are you here?" "It's Monday," I replied. She pauses, "Oh, you didn't get the letter?" Perplexed, I respond, "Huh? What?" She says dryly, "You were laid off."

At once, I fell into a momentary daze and stared at the colorful, bold signs on the wall, "Rise to the Top" and "The Sky is the Limit." The irony of those messages shook me back to awareness. There I was, working on this education project so that students could thrive, soar, and reach their dreams, but honestly, this wasn't my dream. For quite some time, something else had been speaking to me, summoning my soul, a quiet, ongoing whisper that I had been ignoring and doubting. She motions to me, "Turn in your computer."

Suddenly unemployed, sitting in my one-bedroom apartment, I found myself in a valley, a place of deep reflection. Days before, my life had been in continual motion with constant activity. But suddenly, circumstances beyond my control had brought me to a standstill and forced me to stop and think. I was reminded of Iyanla Vanzant's *The Value in the Valley: A Black Woman's Guide Through Life's Dilemmas.* And at that moment, "the valley of purpose and intent" was speaking to me. I was standing, or rather sitting, in the midst of a valley.

Vanzant explains that valleys are places of learning, between the high points and successes, places between the mountains, where we rest, think, and connect with the wisdom within. In the valley of purpose and intent, we dwell there, deeply exploring, to find clarity and commitment to our own purpose.

In the Bible, "the valley" is often referred to as a place where we find spiritual meaning, where our souls come to rest, at low points and at times of challenge and struggle. In the depths of the valley, we call on God with tenacious fervor, reaching out with a piercing clarity, asking God for exactly what we need. It is here, far removed from the comforts of life, where we feel our own longing for God even more deeply and hear the summoning of God even more clearly.

In my own valley, unemployed and untethered, I paid attention to the voice within. This nudge had been speaking to me to take a bold, intentional, and purposeful step forward in my life. My work had been satisfying on some levels, but something else was beckoning me. I had been hosting a women's radio show once a month and absolutely loved interviewing women and shining a light on their stories. I had the idea to branch out to television and produce a show on the local public access station. The idea stayed on the backburner of my mind, ruminating, whispering, and calling, but it wasn't ever really practical. It wouldn't pay the bills. But now, neither did my job, since I no longer had one! As I was sitting on my living room floor, something in me rose up—a summoning and a strong urge to move and act. I jumped up and pulled the DCTV application off the bookshelf. I now had in my hands my next move—clear, committed, and purposeful.

The next day, I turned in my application and joined DCTV, the Public Access Corporation of the District of Columbia. I learned everything I could, took classes, and worked hundreds of volunteer hours on television productions. Finally, I hosted my first television show. In that moment, I felt everything click. I felt a union in my soul, as if everything culminated and converged at once—the creativity, the desire to make a positive impact, and the fulfillment of the calling that had been speaking to my soul. Standing in that television studio, I was filled with an overflowing energy, like I was standing in the center of the very purpose God had ordained.

Beyond the valley, I now stood in a place of purpose. As I was relentlessly volunteering, devoting long hours and much time to this pursuit, it did not solve the issue of "paying the bills." Yet, it was the commitment my soul needed—a solid step forward on the path of purpose, where gifts of the soul align to honor the calling of God. And I was grateful.

For we are His workmanship, created in Christ Jesus for good works, which God prepared beforehand so that we would walk in them.
Ephesians 2:10 NASB1995

When we dwell with Jesus Christ, we possess the knowledge that we are what God has made us and that we have a purpose that God has established long before we even take a single step. The period of coming to that job and gathering experience and skills were all part of the path ... yet so was casting aside that very job. It was part of my path, to dwell in the valley, to hear the summoning of God so clearly, to connect with my own sacred purpose, and walk through the valley to take the next purposeful step on the path God had laid.

The Scripture reminds us that purpose is found and grounded in knowing who and whose we are. To know God created us, as His creation and His workmanship, we serve His purposes when we commit our souls and our works to God. Our purposes—transcending endings and beginnings, situations, and circumstances—orient and pave the path we walk. Truly, your purpose aligns your soul with who God created and called you to be.

On the most fundamental level, our purpose is the reason and the meaning of our existence. In my valley, I sought my own commitment to be on purpose—a meaning that orients everything, that gives the why, the direction, and an unchanging intention that propels my path. While circumstances always change, the steadfastness of God never does. Anchored in Christ, we find our own steadfastness within when we commit to purpose—devoting all of our soul, talents, and works to the path God has prepared for us.

Dwelling in every moment, in every valley, and on every mountaintop, we know that we are created by God for a reason. The purpose may be highly specific—a vocation, career, ministry, or a blessed relationship. Or your purpose may be your own unique, meaningful, and purposeful way of being in the world that brings forth the glory of God through your life. The path of purpose is sacred, walking with God, knowing we hold a purpose in our being that is ordained for good works. When I think of the vastly different people God has created, I am awed by the amazing tapestry of purpose, blessings, and good works God has endowed in and throughout humanity. With your own alignment to what matters most to you—what moves you, excites you, calls you, touches your heart, concerns you, or uses your talents in a way that deeply satisfies and engages you—with a focus on God, you find your highest purpose.

In producing and hosting the television show, I found ways to use the television platform, to be of service, and to do good works. Many amazing women shared their stories, with the television airwaves shining a light on what God had given them, amplifying their good works. When the light and spirit of God flow through us and through our works, that is our crowning moment of purpose.

Life gives us many opportunities to serve, and the world has seemingly endless needs. Your heart, time, and energy can be stretched in many directions. Yet, purpose is not merely found in what is needed by others. Purpose is found in what fills your soul, connects you with God, and lights the path where the grace of God shines through your life. We are a purposeful part of the plan God has ordained. We have a summoning to do good works for the Lord—to bless, touch, love, and impact others with our lives. Wearing the crown of purpose, we hold our heads high. We allow our crowns to guide who we are, what we do, how we move and walk in the world, always and forever glorifying God.

Devotion

Dear God, I dwell in the blessed, sacred knowledge that I am Your creation and Your workmanship. With gratitude, trust, and faith, I walk the path You have ordained for me. I thank you, God, for the purpose You have given me. I call on You as I lift my soul and purpose to You always, to do the good works which glorify Your holy name. I pray for Your light and guidance along the way. I ask You to strengthen and equip me on this path. I thank you for the Spirit of Christ, which fills my soul and lights the way. In Jesus's name, I pray. Thank you, Lord. Amen.

Reflection

Take a few moments to meditate on the Scripture. What does it mean to you, personally, to be God's "workmanship?" Let that truth bathe you completely. Let it be a light that shines within and around you. Write down all that comes up.

Consider deeply your own purpose. Describe what "purpose" means to you and how you express purpose. How does knowing that God prepared a path for you affect how you define your purpose?

Imagine dwelling in a peaceful valley of purpose and intent with God. Bring everything that matters most to you now. Open your soul to His highest truth. What purpose and what path is unfolding before you now?

Write your own devotion here.

Hold it deeply within and say your devotion out loud to God.

Group Discussion

Open with your devotions and reflections on Day 20. What does being committed to purpose mean to you? How does dwelling with Christ impact your purpose? Consider for a moment any "valleys" you have experienced. What did you learn about yourself, God, and your purpose in those moments? For each woman, reflect on the Scripture and discuss how dwelling in the truth, that we are "His workmanship," strengthens your purpose. Close with prayers, lifting up the purpose and calling of each woman to God and His highest purpose for her life.

Day 21

The Uncompromised Mission

I press on toward the goal unto the prize of the high calling of God in Christ Jesus.

Philippians 3:14 ASV

The pastor's words, bold, decisive, and clear, hung in the heat of the summer air, like a rousing call. His words and his message settled into me like a truth that I needed to hear—to not compromise. To not compromise serving Christ, speaking about Christ, loving Christ, and to not compromise our mission and God-given calling. In focused, structured moments of service—a mission trip, a service project, or a vocation—we can be completely devoted to serving God for His highest purposes. Then, the projects, the work, and the moments of service are finished and come to an end. Often, our focus shifts to other concerns, responsibilities, relationships, obligations, and realities. And the mission-driven purpose and divine calling can take a backseat, as other priorities loom larger.

Yet, the pastor's searing sermon stayed with me and challenged me. When I am on mission, whether it be an actual mission trip overseas with a church, or a creative mission, focusing my soul and gifts to be used by God, I am all-in. My mind, body, and spirit are completely and totally focused on being of service. Yet, the sermon pushed me to ask myself: Was I all-in, on mission, *all of the time...* when the project was over, when I exited the church building, or when I returned home? *Truly, was I completely and totally devoted to being on mission and living my calling every moment of my life?*

When I scanned the reality of my life, I realized that in some ways, my life had become compartmentalized. Speaking boldly and freely of the love of God flowed easily and powerfully in some places. In other settings, being more cautious and tentative, not as much. I asked myself: Why do I allow this division and separation? Why do I speak, act, and respond differently in some settings? Does this compromise, in my actions, represent a compromise of my devotion to the calling of God?

Realities of public life impose their own divisions—public versus private, church versus state, religious versus secular. Some settings, such as public sector workplaces that seek the full inclusion, respect, and diversity of all people, have their own norms that determine what speech is permissible. These divisions have affected me personally. I have not always spoken boldly or fully shared my faith nor even explained that my *true* mission and motivations are rooted in the love of Christ, rooted in my connection to God. It has meant speaking of accepted cultural issues in work and social settings, what is commonly and easily shared, yet not going deeper into and revealing my truth. It has meant being less vocal, and even less honest, for fear of being inappropriate, which subtly dims and lowers the light of my truth.

Yet, at some point, considering the ultimate calling of God and purpose of life, I no longer wanted that separation in my consciousness, and in my life, that felt like a compromise in my soul. I no longer wanted to live with this concession: to live sometimes by societal norms and other times by faith. This compromise felt like a watered-down existence, as though I was not truly living and expressing my life purpose fully. To be on a mission in life is a total and complete dedication to purpose. There is no partial or part-time mission. A mission is a purpose that flows through all of life, a total endeavor. It is all-consuming, all-encompassing, all-powerful, and flows through all that we are called to do.

To be on mission flows from following God entirely in all things, in all ways, and at all times. There is no time when the faith is turned off or where the call can be dimmed or diminished. Our mission, our calling, and our divine purpose are continual and unending. It reminds me of the Scripture:

I will the bless the LORD at all times; His praise shall continually be in my mouth.

Psalms 34:1 NASB1995

This Scripture reminds me to speak joyfully of the Lord and live the truth, what God has given me, continually and never ceasing. Like evangelists who believe in the mighty workings of God and share the gospel of Jesus Christ, the praise of God is forever in their hearts, souls, and words. Our missions, too—what God has called us to do—never end. Full devotion is to be fully used, to let there be no place in the consciousness, in the soul, that is not devoted to the mission. Fully devoted, we let no split exist in our mind, thoughts, or belief about what part of our existence is fit for God and what part is not.

Yet, full devotion is a journey, an upward call, through the realities we face in life. It is not necessarily an easy path without snares, valleys, or pitfalls. Life can pull us into different directions, distract us from our mission, and challenge us to reach that complete, uncompromised devotion.

Not that I have already obtained this or have already reached the goal; but I press on to make it my own, because Christ Jesus has made me his own.
Philippians 3:12 NRSV

Accepting and honoring Christ, we know this for sure: We are His. He covers us and claims us. In our devotion to Christ, we have a powerful, illuminating guide as we journey to devote all of our lives to our calling in Christ.

I press on toward the goal unto the prize of the high calling of God in Christ Jesus.
Philippians 3:14 ASV

This devotion steadies us as we face the inevitable challenges in life, which can divide our time, loyalty, and focus. This devotion lets us see clearly the many occasions, opportunities, and circumstances where we may compromise. Yet, it is important to note, compromise is different from finding meaningful common ground with others. Rather, compromise is a costly sacrifice when you surrender or relinquish what is ultimately most important. In those moments and places of compromise, we have space for reflection to ask ourselves—are we giving it all to God, and if not, what is holding us from it?

Life, all of it—our lives, hearts, minds, relationships, and communities—is our mission field. It is our sacred and holy ground. None of life exists outside of the province of God. On this hallowed ground, where God breathes life into each of us, we make our most sacred offering: every part of your life committed to the call of God.

Jesus's words emblazon this truth. When Jesus was approached with the question of paying the tax to Caesar, he asked, *"Whose likeness and inscription is this?"* (Matthew 22:20 NASB1995). It was Caesar's on the coin. And Jesus then replied:

"Then render to Caesar the things that are Caesar's; and to God the things that are God's."
Matthew 22:21 NASB1995

While the inscriptions on coins and currency belong to other authorities, the inscription emblazoned in our hearts and souls belongs to God, as we are made in His image and likeness. Our souls, calling, consciousness, conscience, and mission are fully rendered to the Lord. The world gives us numerous places where different rules, rulers, and authorities govern and apply. But no spiritual authority is higher than God. With an uncompromised devotion to answering the calling God has given you, you are always on mission—all of you, all of the time, serving God.

This uncompromised mission becomes a way of life. There is no place, actual or imagined, where you enter, step forward, and set the calling in your soul aside. To be on a mission is to close any gap between your soul and life, in every moment, and let God lead the way. We tear down any division within, any parts of ourselves walled off, cut off, or held apart from God, either in mind or in reality. We offer ourselves fully to God, to a missionary path of overflowing blessings, where the glory of God can permeate, break through and shine through any and every moment of our lives.

There is power in your calling—the full, unfettered, undivided energy flowing to a mighty purpose. Compromised, we diminish what can be done in our lives. Uncompromised, you give your soul over to God fully, engaging the full power of your soul to serve God without limit.

In service to His creation, giving ourselves totally to His mission, we truly do God's work in and through our lives. To say, unlimited and uncompromised, "Yes!" with all your soul to God, you answer your call and fulfill your highest, blessed, and most sacred mission.

Devotion

Dear God, I present every moment of my life to You—the moments when I am bold, filled with faith, and on mission, and the moments when I am not. I ask for Your grace and guidance to steady me, speak to me, and hold me in every moment. In my upward call, I fully devote all my soul, life, and calling to You. I thank you, God, for Jesus Christ, for His standard, His love, and His truth, in which I find restoration and light. I offer my mission to You, devoting all for Your magnificence, glory, and grace to shine in our world. In Your holy name, I pray. Amen.

Reflection

Take a few moments to reflect on a time when you were fully "on mission" serving God. What did that moment feel like? What was most meaningful to you? How can you expand that devotion? Write down all that comes up.

Consider a time, if any, where it felt like you "compromised" your truth, expression of faith, or calling. What did you learn in that moment? How can that insight propel deeper devotion?

Take a few minutes to reflect on "successes" on the path that is your mission. Now, consider at least one major "challenge." Imagine the grace of God within you, flowing to, through, and around you with every step. What do you know for sure about your journey with God?

Write your own devotion here.

Hold it deeply in your soul and say your devotion aloud to God as a prayer.

Group Discussion

Open with your devotions and take 10 minutes for meditation, reflecting on the question: What do you know for sure about your journey with God? Share your reflections on the meditation and insights on Day 21. What does it mean to be fully devoted to the mission of God at all times? What challenges and opportunities does this full devotion present? Now, consider: What does it cost you to *not* be fully and constantly devoted in your calling to God? For each woman, share encouragement to propel each other on your upward call. Close with prayers of devotion and strength, lifting up the mission of each woman to God.

THEME EIGHT

Overflowing: The Supremacy of Love

Love is the greatest power in humanity—a boundless force that connects us at the soul level, to each other, and to all of creation. Love, unlimited in its reach and infinite in its capacities, is our own God-given expression of grace. Love flows as a gift we give to one another and to ourselves, an unending portal of God's grace that overflows through the world. In Scripture and in the depth of our souls, we know the power of this love. As God gave His only begotten Son for all humanity, we feel the depth of God's love deep in our spirits. To take hold of this overflowing love, we must claim the full power and potential of what this love can do.

In your calling, God equips you uniquely. Yet, love is the energy, the God-given grace overflowing that undergirds your calling, expands its power, and opens it for the love of God to shine gloriously. While love can be passive, receptively, and graciously received, love is also ours to give actively, wield intentionally, and share expansively, as you walk your own sacred God-given path. In these next three days, we explore this love—the love we give to others, the love we give ourselves, and the boundless possibilities for the communities we love.

Day 22

To Wield the Power of Love

"You shall love the Lord your God with all your heart, and with all your soul, and with all your mind, and with all your strength.' The second is this, 'You shall love your neighbor as yourself.' There is no other commandment greater than these."

Mark 12:30-31 NRSV

Imagine living thousands of years ago, when Jesus lived and walked the earth. You can come face to face with the Lord, breath to breath, and ask Him anything. You could instantly know the answers to what you have always longed to know. Time after time, I have prayed to God, "Please, give me the direction, show me what I must do now, please show me the way." If I could be present with Jesus, I imagine glimpsing the magnitude of Him and beholding the mystery of God and of all creation. I imagine, I would set aside my limited view of life and the particularity of my personal questions. I can imagine, I would simply ask, *"What would you tell me, Lord?"*

The disciples, the women, and the men Jesus encountered had the opportunity to speak to Him and ask questions. Some, seeking to both test Jesus and know his wisdom asked, "Which commandment is the first of all?" (Mark 12:28 NRSV). Jesus answered, revealing all my soul would ever seek to know: *to love.* To love God absolutely, with every aspect of your being, your heart, your soul, your mind, and your strength, and to love your neighbor as yourself.

The year after I was baptized, I was on a mission to share *love.* After many evenings in an evangelism course, I had passion, pamphlets, and a message in my heart to share the gospel and the love of Jesus Christ. I shared the message with people I encountered, whether I was chatting casually at a restaurant or with the young neighbors who frequently gathered in front of my home. Those conversations were enlivening—I felt a true connection with Christ, the message of salvation, and love connected me with every human soul. No one was a stranger; everyone was united in God's love.

One evening, a friend arranged a meeting for me with a war veteran, whom I had never met, to help me with the lyrics for a song I was writing. I was grateful to meet Jay, and I was genuinely thankful for his kindness. He eagerly volunteered to review my song about a veteran suffering from inner pain. As Jay read the lyrics, he began to open up and shared how painful his experience had been while serving in the war. Despite his warm, friendly exterior, I could feel his pain, a deep heaviness in his heart. He confided that he had suffered from post-traumatic stress syndrome and had buried many hurtful things.

I felt an overwhelming compassion, yet also a clear awareness that there was nothing I could say to ease all those years of buried pain. Yet, I also felt a love I needed to share. I asked him, then, if he knew Jesus. Jay shared that because he was gay, he didn't feel that he could go to church, so he stayed away. I felt his inner turmoil meeting this larger cultural and religious conflict. Yet, at that moment, I felt his pain as if it was my own. It was just the two of us, one with a heart deeply wounded, and one with a heart carrying an unfailing belief in the love and power of Jesus Christ. I felt compelled to bridge this gap, between him and healing, between his heart and the love of Christ.

I wanted him to know and be touched by the deepest, most compassionate, most inextinguishable love that exists: *the love of Jesus Christ.* I wanted him to encounter this love in a way that would touch his heart, heal his pain, and soothe the suffering in his soul. With his generosity, Jay blessed me, a total stranger with a need. I thanked Jay with all my heart, and I encouraged him. And that evening, I prayed for him that the overflowing love of Christ would surround him, comfort him, and draw him closer to God.

Jay, his heart, his pain, and his conflict stayed with me. On this path to share the love of Christ, I realized I would encounter the full gamut of humanity, moving headlong into pain and profound possibilities, crossing personal, cultural, and ideological boundaries. These encounters open up sacred spaces where people share the depths of who they are, and in that space, we have a sacred calling—to share love. This is the love I embraced in my soul when I said yes to Jesus Christ. This is the love that forever buoys me and guides my soul. This is the love–and the answer—for all I encounter on my path. To meet a wide-open heart and share love is to sow love into the sacred ground of human souls where the love of Christ overflows and does its work. Truly, when you are filled with the love of Christ, it becomes a charge, a sacred duty, to share love. And, the words of Jesus make this clear:

"You shall love the Lord your God with all your heart, and with all your soul, and with all your mind, and with all your strength.' The second is this, 'You shall love your neighbor as yourself.' There is no other commandment greater than these."

Mark 12:30-31 NRSV

Love becomes a blessing, a power, a sacred way of being in the world. Jesus Christ embodied total, absolute, and undying love for the lives and the souls of all humanity. He gives us the command to fully absorb the love of God into our being, with a forceful intensity from the heart, mind, soul, and strength. Then, the command to love our neighbors takes this love and spreads it deep, far, and wide, way beyond our own personal boundaries. While the love we feel toward our children, friends, spouses, and family is personal, our neighbors—those who God commands us to love—can be absolutely anyone. This love lies beyond the direct, important ties of our personal connections and daily obligations. This love, limitless and unconditional, calls us into the wide-open, loving embrace of *all* people on God's earth.

Love becomes a way of touching all humankind. Grounded in this love, carrying this love, we have the invitation to search the depths of our own callings. You have the opportunity to find, enter into, and stand in the places where this love moves through you. Jesus's love worked miracles, healed what had never been healed, raised people back to life, pulled people out of sorrow, and opened closed eyes to the fullness and promise of a glorious new day. Being filled with the love of Christ, we share the miraculous potential to impact one another. To touch someone, to hear their pain, and to respond with love—love overflows.

Love becomes a power, a sacred gift, and a blessing. To hold love in our beings, completely and intentionally, we share love as a purposeful force. To share love boldly, the love of Christ expands endlessly—healing, transforming, breaking down walls, and bringing people closer to God. We can choose to grow strong in this love, as we give love, think in love, respond with love, and speak love. With love, we are equipped to meet every circumstance and truly embrace every neighbor on our path.

Love orients our calling. We become agents, intercessors, and portals of grace, wherever we are and whenever love is needed. In the beautiful synchronicity of this glorious design of God's encounters, the love we carry within us is often precisely what someone else might desperately need. Love becomes a force that draws your heart, pulls your passion, and moves you toward others. Love becomes a sacred power that we wield—we *decide* to love. We can decide to let love rule and reign, share it fearlessly and compassionately, and let God's love be overflowing in all we are called to do.

Now, going back to that imaginary conversation with Jesus, who already knows the places your soul is needed, the path you walk, and all the steps you take ... imagine the landscape of your calling. Consider all that is in your sight and on your path, every person in your midst, everything you hold in your hands, and all the unchartered territory. Now imagine standing with the Lord and asking the question you most deeply want to know. For all our questions, our purposes, and all we are called to do, we have a blessed command and a sacred power—to love.

Devotion

Dear God, I open my heart, my soul, and my mind to You. I pray that Your love flows through me like a mighty current, washing away any fears and pulsating through me as a force of goodness and grace. May Your love guide my steps, my thoughts, and the words I say. I pray that Your love gives me courage and strengthens me. Let me see my neighbors and everyone as You see them. Dear Lord, let me be Your hands and feet, touching others so they may feel, know, and be blessed by Your love. May Your glorious love overflow in every moment and in every place you have placed me. In Jesus's name, I pray. Amen.

Reflection

Take 10 minutes and meditate on the Scripture for Day 22. Before you begin, hold this question in your heart, soul, mind, and intention: What is love calling me to do? Write down all that you feel and receive.

Consider your heart deeply. What moves your heart? What are you most drawn to? How do you share love? What matters most to you? Be specific as possible.

Now imagine being filled by the love of Christ. How can the love of Christ propel your calling even further? How, and with whom, can you share love even more expansively? How could love flow even more powerfully through you?

Write your own devotion here.

Let the words fill your heart, mind, your soul, and your strength.

Group Discussion

Open with your devotions and reflections on Day 22. Begin with the question: If there were absolutely no limits on what you could do, what would you do empowered with boundless love? How would this affect your purpose and calling? How would this love impact your relationships and your encounters with everyone you meet? How can a deeper love expand what God has called you to do? How does this love grow you and enlarge the territory you touch? For each woman, share at least one specific action you will take. Close with prayer, powerfully lifting up each woman's heart, mind, and soul to be filled and expanded by the love of God.

Day 23

To Commune in the Circle of Love

Above all, clothe yourselves with love, which binds everything together in perfect harmony.

Colossians 3:14 NRSV

In communion, the sacred and tender gathering of sisters and brothers, coming together in the spirit of remembrance of Jesus Christ, we break bread as one body. Communion knits the hearts of each person together in a sacred purpose that transcends the singular moment of the ritual. This shared love harmonizes the needs, hearts, and gifts of many different people and overflows—lifting us, sustaining us, and binding us all together.

The evening before my grandfather's funeral, we sat circled at the shiny wooden dining room table at my grandparents' home. With my grandma and "Gemma," a stalwart, elder member of the church, we shared precious memories and talked about the service the next day. The warmth and energy of our gathering felt like a warm, comforting light through my sadness. Then, after more than an hour of talking, Gemma suddenly announced, with clarity and duty, she had to go home and cook the chicken for the repast the next day. I admired her sense of responsibility to visit with us, then jump into action to do her "best soul food cooking" so that we would all be well fed after the funeral service.

The next day, at the repast, there was a glorious spread to serve hundreds of people. As the sumptuous aroma of Gemma's lovingly prepared fried chicken floated into the room, it seemed to bring joy to those who were eating. My only regret—I had stopped eating meat! So, I could not partake, and it smelled so good! When I walked back into the kitchen, the small area was brimming with focused and organized activity. Several women were prepping food, and a teenage boy and girl I didn't know, too young to have ever met my grandfather, were busy at work. I witnessed a community of love, people springing into action, serving, and uplifting others in their time of need. I was grateful to be lovingly embraced by this circle, by this church, and by the hearts of these people giving what they could.

I saw love in action, a broad *agape* love that flows through compassion, kindness, and the service of people coming together in a shared purpose. That day at the funeral, my heart was raw, open, yearning, and grateful. Every hug felt like an inpouring of warmth that filled my spirit. Every tender word lifted my heart, and every kind act felt like the love of Christ circling and embracing me when I needed it most. Our shared purpose that day, harmonized by the love of Christ, surrounded us and pulled all of our hearts together.

Above all, clothe yourselves with love, which binds everything together in perfect harmony. And let the peace of Christ rule in your hearts, to which indeed you were called in one body. And be thankful.

Colossians 3:14-15 NRSV

I was grateful for the community of people who pulled together. It was the kind of love and shared community within which I could rest, be weak and vulnerable, be cared for, and tended to. I felt a love, blessed and overflowing, a communion that transcended the church we shared and that special moment. It was a love that stayed with me and let me see the power, grace, and the lasting legacy of what the love of people coming together for one purpose can do.

Outside of those church walls, divides and barricades, whether ethnicity, culture, race, nationality, and even religion, separate people. We often stand apart, divided into our own needs, agendas, and priorities. Yet, the spirit of Christ, which called us into one body, flows in love that moves through and undergirds all life. This love rescues us during disasters, from the catastrophic to the personal, when you simply need someone to lean on. This love sweetly watches over the elderly neighbor, supports a friend struggling with a heavy load, and moves us triumphantly through painful conflicts.

In a crisis, when the conditions of our lives break down—a death, a sudden tragedy, an unexpected twist on the road of life—we are jolted into the sudden, clear awareness of what is most important. It's ironic, but this is often where love flourishes. When the divisions between people fall away, the urgent—what matters most—rises clearly and profoundly, and the distance between people closes. In this clear call, and with this certain purpose, love rises.

In this time, we put on love, the shining imprint of who we really are, and express love through a shared purpose that beautifully harmonizes us. This love of Christ dwells in the spirit and flows between us, transcending boundaries of class, culture, language, and oceans. We can choose and join into this love with each other. The love of Christ is an invitation to enter into, reside in, and commune in love. Finding love in a community may not always be easy, particularly where there are differences and hurts, but the force of love created through a single, shared purpose is undeniable. We can commune within this circle of love, fully aware of all the pitfalls and despair, yet appreciate the blessed ties that bind us.

In our callings, we have choices and opportunities that rest on our own initiative. And in this human collective, we are intertwined within this web of love. We can tap into this love, embrace and cultivate it, serve and contribute to it, and strengthen this love. Through this lens of love, we value what we offer, appreciate what others bring, and step forward in love.

We witness how the love of Christ holds the highest purpose, weaving the gifts, contributions, offerings, needs, and even the hurts, of many people together. We see how love moves through pain and challenges and reconciles us to God and to each other. We see the grandest reaches of what we can be and what is truly possible within the sacred circle of love. In whatever way God touches your heart, it is a sacred call to honor this extraordinary love, appreciate it, and let it be the foundation of all that God has called you to be and do. We can let love drive, fuel, enliven, enrich, and propel our calling—what moves uniquely in your heart and soul.

Many years have passed since my grandfather's funeral service. The dear people who worked in the kitchen, and the teenagers who are now adults, have no idea the impression they left with me. Their loving actions that day filled my heart with a cherished, everlasting memory. And Gemma, with her incredible sense of duty and superb fried chicken, showed the power of responding to the call, in her own unique way, with love.

Love flows supremely. There is no place it cannot touch. Being attuned to this love, we invite it in and through us in every possible way and moment. Whether working in a group, a mission, or in your own creative solitude, *love connects us.* Whenever, wherever, or however we are called, as we move and commune in love, we are enlarged by the love of Christ.

We make a sacred choice to embrace this love, to join with others in a circle of love, and see God in each other. Through a lens of love, you can choose to align your heart, your thoughts, and view your possibilities, challenges, and all those you encounter with love. With love flowing through your gifts, talents, service, and work, you expand and enrich the circle of love. In that sacred communion of life, the love, blessing, and grace of God overflow. Tap into the love within the deepest reach of your soul that energizes your heart. Bring this love, your passion, and your calling into the sacred circle of love, and let your love be overflowing in our world.

Devotion

Dear God, I come before You with gratitude and a powerful and clear awareness that we are all connected in Your love. I pray that everything You have placed in my soul, heart, and calling will be harmonized in Your love. I ask for Your blessed guidance on the path I walk in life and to let me see the beauty, grace, and blessing of being in this circle of love. May the love of Christ draw my heart into communion with Your highest purpose and every soul You place on my path. I am eternally grateful for Your love that connects, guides, and overflows. In Jesus' name, I pray. Amen.

Reflection

Think of a community, a group, or family of which you are a member that is meaningful to you. Imagine the love of Christ and the power of all His love can do, touching and expanding in your midst. What images, possibilities, and vision do you hold for this group? Write down all that comes up.

Now imagine the love of Christ touching you powerfully, flowing through your gifts, and overflowing in your heart. How can you share love and act with love in this group?

Now, contemplate the power of your calling within a circle of love, love that flows through you, Christ, and everybody. How does this love inform, inspire, and guide your calling?

Write your own devotion here.

Let the words and love expand in your heart and lift your voice in prayer.

Group Discussion

Open with your devotions and share your insights and personal reflections on Day 23. How has being in a circle of love, a communion of people, blessed you? What meant the most to you in that experience? How have you been a blessing to others within a group, community, or circle of love? Share examples of harmony—how have you witnessed the love of people coming together? What was the impact? How can holding this lens of love strengthen your purpose and calling? Close with statements, one powerful word (or a few): what will you share in this circle of love? End with a prayer circle, lifting up each woman in the harmony of God's love.

Day 24

To Revive Yourself in Love

I pray that you may have the power to comprehend, with all the saints, what is the breadth and length and height and depth, and to know the love of Christ that surpasses knowledge, so that you may be filled with all the fullness of God.

Ephesians 3:18-19 NRSV

To come to Christ with your heart wide open, your soul fully devoted, and your life fully surrendered to His sacred way, you will know the unsurpassable love of God—deeply, divinely, and personally. This love, boundless and infinite, is yours to receive freely. This love becomes a force that sustains, orients, drives, and lifts you and all that you do. In serving Christ, devoting ourselves and our callings to sharing the love of Christ, our focus is often on the well-being and welfare of others. We lift people up. We minister, teach, soothe, help, create, lead, solve and resolve. We sincerely attune to people and attend to their needs. We see them compassionately—we see Christ in them—and we love freely.

In serving, we give, give, and give even more. There is always a need in the world, a place, a person, a situation where the penetrating need for love beckons. I often pray, *"Use me, Lord."* I love that prayer, surrendering myself, asking for the mighty grace and power of God to work through all that I am, wherever I am, according to the His glorious will. *"Yes, Lord, let Your will be done."* Yet, at times, I need to *rest*. I need to receive an inpouring of God's love and bask in His love. Simply, I need to take time to be filled by love ... and to love myself.

It is a mighty and important calling to be a bountiful blessing to others, to give your energy, love, and attention to family, neighbors, community, and those you work with and serve. Yet, all that loving, serving, and stepping up, can take you to the precipice of your own personal limits. There, we often teeter in the shadows of weariness and exhaustion. Unwittingly, or even intentionally, we can sacrifice ourselves in service to others by not acknowledging and attending to our own vital needs, commitments, and desires. The result is often pain—physical and emotional—and feelings of personal neglect.

At those times, we must compassionately recognize our own needs for love, balance, sustenance, and well-being. We often need a loving reminder. As you mightily serve God, devoting yourself on the mission field of life, you too profoundly deserve the love you so freely share with others.

Our loving regard for ourselves and our callings are intertwined, each needing love and attention, thereby fueling the other. Yet, it took me a while to really get this. I remember once, while working in my 20s, I was coordinating a project and became so immersed in getting things done that I routinely worked through lunch. A coworker reminded me, "You know, you can eat lunch. The work will still be there." I laughed, thinking, this is simply how I work.

Yet, one day, while planning a date for a major leadership meeting and juggling the schedules of the entire team, I looked at the calendar, saw my long-standing doctor appointment, and thought, "I'll just move it, reschedule my appointment, and then, we can meet that day."

Much later, when talking to team members and hearing them discuss their personal lives, I realized that everyone else had commitments and obligations that they honored. Sure, I had youthful naivete and serious determination to do an excellent job, yet that experience was a significant lesson. Although my role was central to the entire project, I was easily and casually willing to sidestep my own needs and negotiate the priority of my own health. I had not placed a firm, loving regard on my own needs, nor had I established what was essential for me—what I needed for my own well-being.

In some ways, this incident was minor, yet its impact was enduring. Imagine how not regarding your own needs can become a problematic pattern in the face of competing duties and responsibilities. We can become so mission-focused, so driven to serve others, that tending to ourselves could even be considered selfish or unimportant. So, you compromise yourself, neglect your own needs, drain your energy, and deplete your capacity to fulfill your *own* calling. Yet, when you consider the magnitude of all that God is and all that God has called you to be and do, the love you give yourself is *essential.*

When we allow ourselves to bask in the love of God freely and completely, without reservation or limitation, we choose to let ourselves be loved and filled. We have from the Scripture the beautiful words:

> *I pray that you may have the power to comprehend, with all the saints, what is the breadth and length and height and depth, and to know the love of Christ that surpasses knowledge, so that you may be filled with all the fullness of God.*
> *Ephesians 3:18-19 NRSV*

When I open up myself to know the love of Christ, I enter into a place of unimaginable love, feeling, and seeing all that love can do.

I ponder Christ's eternal and undying compassion for humanity. This love becomes a fuel that flows into and sustains us. We can say yes, to consciously receiving love, and importantly, giving this love to ourselves. Resting in love, we dwell closer, more intimately with God, and connect even more deeply to the love within us.

To actively love yourself extends the love of Christ to yourself. It is paramount for your nourishment, life, mission, and soul to not deny yourself the love that is yours to receive. When you fully allow love in, you become an open vessel. Blockages, resistance, and hindrances dissolve, and God's love flows to and from you gloriously. To uphold love for yourself and your own well-being, you nurture and steward the calling God has placed in your heart.

As we tend to ourselves with loving regard, we engender a deeper appreciation for our own mission. We become more closely attuned to the interflow of love—how love sustains us, flows from God, and drives everything we do. When women love themselves and their calling, it is no trite matter. We become powerfully aware of our purposes and how we intentionally invest ourselves, our time, and our energy. We love and honor what God has given us to be and do. And as we emanate love, as we endow our lives and paths as worthy, the love around us expands.

This love becomes a lens, a fullness of being, to reconcile, to align, and devote your choices and decisions to what God has called you. This love empowers your ongoing walk with God, as the magnificent glory of God shines on your sacred path. Therefore, to love yourself is ultimate—never to be diminished, ignored, or sacrificed.

With glorious self-love, we lessen the possibilities of self-neglect and pour our love into what matters most. We reduce the risk of weariness, running ourselves down, and sacrificing our health and well-being. We strengthen our capacity to share the love of Christ in all that we are and in all our blessed purposes.

Love makes your path sacred. To love yourself, to let every part of you be filled with the love of Christ is to be revived in His overflowing love. Gloriously and completely, let this love powerfully flow through you, all that you do, and every aspect, fiber, and expression of the woman God called to you be.

Devotion

Dear God, I open myself to You, fully—my mind, heart, body, and soul without hesitation, reservation, or limitation. I ask to receive Your love fully—to be filled abundantly. Please restore the places in me that have been hurt, worn, and need Your gracious love. I pray that Your love strengthens me as I lovingly care for myself. May Your love guide all that You have placed in my hand and heart—my calling, relationships, family, community, and service. I am eternally grateful for Your love that uplifts me and overflows. With boundless love, I thank you, God. Amen.

Reflection

Take 10 minutes, breathe deeply and relax. Imagine and contemplate the love of Christ flowing to and through you, filling you, touching you completely. Ponder this love deeply in your heart. What did this love feel like?

Reflecting on the meditation above, focus on your thoughts and actions toward yourself. How freely and easily do you love yourself? What does it mean to you to love yourself?

Now, consider deeply: How does your love of yourself open you to be filled with the love of Christ? Does anything hinder this flow of love? How might you increase this flow of love?

Write your own devotion here.

Hold it deeply in your heart and speak it aloud to God as a prayer.

Group Discussion

Open with sharing your devotions and set the intention for open and honest expression. Share your reflections and insights from Day 24. What does it mean to truly let the love of Christ fill you? Why is this love so essential to feel personally? Why is loving yourself important for your calling? Consider any blockades to receiving the love of Christ and loving yourself fully. Where do these hindrances come from, and how can you remove them? For each woman, share how you strengthen your own self-love and why it matters. Close with prayers of love, lifting each woman up to be filled with the love of Christ.

THEME NINE

Honor the Voice of Your Soul

In stillness, in the blessed inhale and exhale of your own breath, lies a sacred sound—the voice of your soul. This voice, lying far deeper than the words you speak, is the truth within you. The voice of your soul moves and speaks through your passions and convictions, your deepest loves and most abiding faith, your clearest visions, and your own very connection with God. Yet, this voice, not always the loudest, sometimes whispers and sometimes shouts, is the voice we must learn to hear and honor.

Many voices surround us that influence culture, society, religion, beliefs, and even our own consciousness. Yet, to hear your own voice, in the midst of it all, is to trust what you hear most deeply within you—to trust what flows from your soul. With trust, you honor what moves you, what matters to you, and all that God has endowed within you to live, breathe, and speak into existence.

In these next three days, we honor the voice of your soul—the truth within you, the depth of its boldness, and the blessings that overflow when you embody and give voice to all that God has bestowed in your own glorious and sacred voice.

Day 25

Let Your Truth Be Spoken

At this point His disciples came, and they were amazed that He had been speaking with a woman, yet no one said, "What do You seek?" or, "Why do You speak with her?"

John 4:27 NASB1995

He encountered her—a woman considered an outcast to most, devalued and diminished by the prevailing standards of her times. Yet, there she stood. With a past filled with five husbands, this Samaritan woman stood with Him. The simple act of meeting a stranger at a well would, ordinarily, be quite common. Yet, this encounter—a woman talking directly to Jesus, God in the flesh amongst us—was extraordinary.

Jesus's disciples watched as His conversation with this woman ripped right through the tightly bound customs of their society, which excluded and limited women to specific roles and spheres. His conversation lifted her beyond all cultural limits and drew her immediately into a divine relationship. Jesus Christ revealed to her: *"...but those who drink of the water that I will give them will never be thirsty. The water that I will give will become in them a spring of water gushing up to eternal life." (John 4:14 NRSV).*

The woman, eagerly thirsting, asked for the water of which He spoke, yet Jesus gave her even more. Hearing Him speak of the events of her past life, unknowable to a mere man, she realized she was talking to a prophet. She told him of how her ancestors worshiped on the mountain, and Jesus gave her this eternal truth: "*God is spirit, and those who worship him must worship in spirit and truth." (John 4:24 NRSV)*. She told him of her faith and her belief that the Messiah is coming. In that eternally profound moment, Jesus revealed himself directly to her: "*...I am he, the one who is speaking to you." (John 4:26 NRSV)*. Breaking through all walls of societal separation, Jesus Christ gave the divine revelation directly and personally to *her*—a woman at a well.

She was changed. Filled and overflowing with the Spirit of the eternal water in her soul, she left and boldly raised her voice. Speaking the truth of her spectacular, life-changing experience, she proclaimed: *"Come and see a man who told me everything I have ever done! He cannot be the Messiah, can he?" (John 4:29 NRSV)*. She encountered God and now spoke with the authority of the truth that flowed in her soul.

This holy conversation, Jesus and the woman at the well, holds so much power. It was counter-cultural, revolutionary for Jesus to even *speak* to this Samaritan woman. Yet, her personal history and social standing would not separate her from God. His words with her signaled a blessed, social upheaval. God manifested as "man" on earth, as Jesus Christ, acknowledged and listened to the voice of this woman. Their conversation was personal and engaging. He spoke, and she listened. She asked, and He answered. Her voice was present with God. Yet, although they were astonished as they watched, Jesus's disciples kept their silence:

At this point His disciples came, and they were amazed that He had been speaking with a woman, yet no one said, "What do You seek?" or, "Why do You speak with her?"
John 4:27 NASB1995

In their sacred conversation, with the wisdom and revelation therein, we get an answer to the question—*Why do you speak with her?* She is not below anyone. She is worthy of being with Him, entirely in His presence, and being in holy conversation with Jesus Christ. She mattered to God, a beloved woman made in the image of the Almighty God. The substance, the meaning, and expression of her personhood mattered. Her life, her soul, and her voice mattered to God.

The sacred act of coming face to face and speaking with God imparted a truth in her being. She received a message emanating from her own lived experience that she had to tell. Her voice carried a sacred calling—to honor what Jesus had spoken straight into her soul. She left the encounter overflowing, touched by the power of God, and filled with a desire to tell her truth.

She raised her voice and shared the news of Jesus Christ for everyone to hear: *From that city many of the Samaritans believed in Him because of the word of the woman who testified, "He told me all the things that I have done." (John 4:39* NASB1995*).* Her voice moved people to action—birthing a spiritual transformation for those who believed and heard the truth of her testimony. The woman at the well honored the voice of her soul and spoke her truth.

We must speak the truth God gives us. Truly, our voices overflow with the power God bestows when we seek truth, hear it, and honor it. We have a blessed opportunity to speak directly with God in our own sacred communion and bring the substance and depth of our lives into His holy presence. When you give voice to your experience, who you are, what matters to you, what moves you—you honor what God has placed in your soul to speak into existence. Through your voice, you can sow love, create new ways of thinking and living, and bring forth your most magnificent and glorious vision.

To speak your truth is a sacred calling—to go deep within and unleash the power of your God-given voice. In our prayers and conscious thoughts, we enter into a holy conversation with God. In receptivity and with purpose, you can hear God and your own voice more clearly and choose to honor what comes forth. To honor the voice of your soul is to acknowledge what is crucial in your soul—all that you must speak into our world and all God has imparted to you. When we express what we know, understand, feel, and envision, we blaze new pathways as we are called to do.

Like the woman at the well, we tap into His living water and draw the power of Christ into our souls. Overflowing with living water, your voice becomes a mighty force. God has always heard women's voices, and women's voices have always been needed, necessary, and transformational in our world. You have the sacred call to honor your voice and share your truth boldly. To say definitively, resolutely, authoritatively, what I have to say matters. My voice and my truth will be spoken.

Your God-given voice radiates light and fills the pivotal pieces in society that God is sketching, forming, reforming, creating, and revealing through your own sacred calling. Your voice, and all it touches, shapes the world, an ever-unfolding creation, as it carries the honored message God has given you. Ultimately, it is your calling to give voice to everything that flows from the depths of your soul, being, and life. We have a well, the overflowing power of God, to draw from that raises and uplifts our voices and all that God has called us to bring forth.

That conversation at the well—Jesus with the Samaritan woman—broke barriers for millennia to come. Being neither a queen nor a noble, she was simply, yet remarkably, a beloved woman who talked to God. Honor your voice, all that is growing, flowing, and overflowing, because it is yours. Truly and profoundly, you have a God-given truth that must be spoken.

Devotion

Dear God, to You, I lift up my voice and open my soul. I thank you for our sacred communion. Fill my soul with the waters of Your truth and my heart with Your love. Infuse my mind with Your clarity and enlarge my imagination with Your most glorious vision. I pray for Your grace and steady hand as I live, breath, and speak into existence what You called me to bring forth. I pray that my soul carries the love and light of Your truth. I pray that my voice overflows with the power of Your glorious name. In Jesus's name, I pray. Amen.

Reflection

We often come to God, seeking to hear assurance, peace, and direction. Now, contemplate deeply in your heart, mind, and soul the other part of the conversation—your voice. What do you believe God desires to hear from you? What do you feel compelled to say to God? Write down all that comes up.

Search your soul deeply and take a few minutes to ponder: What do you believe God has entrusted within your soul—that must be spoken through your life? What is your soul urging you to share?

Now imagine being filled by the overflowing love and power of Christ flowing through your soul, your voice, and the words you speak. What purpose do you feel within? What has God called you to give voice to in your territory—your mission, community, and world? Write down all that you hear and pray for guidance to bring it forth.

Write your own devotion here.

Speak it out loud to God as your powerful testimony and prayer.

Group Discussion

Open with your devotions and reflections on Day 25. Begin with the question: What does it mean to truly listen to and hear your own voice? Share examples. Do you recognize your own voice as powerful and necessary? Why or why not? For each woman: What does it mean to you to honor the voice of your soul? Consider, if God works through every woman: How does speaking your truth and sharing your experience fill in a part of God's creation? To close, what is your soul calling you to speak now? End with prayers of strength—lifting and blessing the soul, voice, and calling of each woman.

Day 26

Let Your Soul be Bold

On the day I called, You answered me; You made me bold with strength in my soul.

Psalms 138:3 NASB1995

A pulsing drumbeat moved within her, pushing her to step where she had never stepped before—into freedom. Isabella lived within the painful confines of slavery, where her brothers and sisters were sold off to slaveholders miles away. She endured excruciating beatings that left her skin lacerated and bloody with scars. This oppression was her life, yet it was not her choice. Often, she would go away to a private place and pray aloud to God to help her find a better place to be.

One still dawn, before the sun had risen, she stood solemnly and weighed a decision in her mind. She had been taught as a slave to "obey," even to a brutal master. Now, holding her infant daughter, Isabella took her first step out of bondage. No one pursued her, and she walked into the glorious sunlight. She eventually found safe harbor in a home of kind souls. One year later, she was granted legal freedom. Finally, Isabella was free, and she changed her name to the woman God called her to be: Sojourner Truth.

As I read the *Narrative of Sojourner Truth*, the boldness and wisdom of her voice, which transcends times and circumstances, overflows and inspires me to this day. The boldness of a soul powered by God speaks loudly. She possessed a conscience and strong inner voice that even slavery could not vanquish. Sojourner spoke as though her very soul was tethered to the sovereignty of God, seared to the protection of the Lord. In her tightly held and constant prayer, she called on God with powerful certainty. She was anchored to a force that could never be owned, denied, or suppressed—the boldness of her own soul with God.

Her bold soul became a palpable force that fueled her voice and her divine mission. She would go on to raise her voice, raising the consciousness of a nation, speaking courageously with conviction to the horrors of slavery and the dignity of all life. Her voice, impacting generations, powered by the Almighty, brings to life the Scripture in Psalms—spoken and embodied:

On the day I called, You answered me; You made me bold with strength in my soul.
Psalms 138:3 NASB1995

This prayer of calling out to God invokes the life of Sojourner Truth and countless women around the world, throughout time, who embodied the undeniable power of being with God. Women—steeped with strength in their soul—carry on, take the next step, and do what must be done. To know, without a doubt, that the Almighty hears and strengthens you builds a sacred and profound relationship. This inner connection compels you to honor the stirrings in your soul and empowers your sacred calling.

In Sojourner Truth's account, she presents a spiritual truth revealed through her life, an enslaved woman who searched for her *own* answers within. While still enslaved, she contemplated injustice, the slaveholder's broken promise that he would grant her freedom. She considered the risk and the ultimate danger of what escape could bring upon her. Yet, her voice, the weight of her own conscience and soul, was stronger, and it prevailed. This remarkably bold voice came not from any earthly or man-made authority but from her own soul. Her deeply held belief in God's omnipresence and providence was unwavering. She spoke from the depths of a soul anchored in God, unmovably connected to a transcendent force, more profound and powerful than anything on earth.

To be anchored with God is to know God is with you. This anchor so deeply connects your soul and mind to the unlimited power and breadth of God that it sustains, lifts, and propels you. Securely grounded, anchored in the depth of your being, your voice flows with boldness and power. God gives us a voice for a divine purpose—to bring forth a divine mission.

On one occasion, Sojourner's voice and boldness were tested. While at a revival to share the message of God, an angry mob of men arrived. Sojourner was initially overtaken with fear, being the lone black person there. She leaned into her faith, telling herself she, a servant of God, shall not hide and will be protected. She stepped forward and sang about the resurrection of Jesus Christ. As the menacing crowd closed in, she addressed them directly and spoke boldly. Her voice and words changed the very atmosphere. As though sensing the power in the air, what could have been violence was not. The rioters left, and her message of God prevailed.

Sojourner famously raised her voice, with God-given boldness, as a sacred responsibility. She broke more barriers that had limited humanity, calling on the power of women in her now-famous speech at the Women's Rights Convention in 1851:

"If the first woman God ever made was strong enough to turn the world upside down all alone, these women together ought to be able to turn it back, and get it right side up again!"

This turning of phrase, reimagining, and speaking for human possibilities was bold and visionary. She exhorted women to use their God-given ability to do all they can do. A formerly enslaved woman, who relied on God to walk to freedom, spoke into the world a new narrative about the Bible, God, and possibilities for women that holds power to this very day. She presents an empowering truth: Women, together with God, are a powerful and mighty force.

It's a sacred act to honor the voice of your own soul, every magnificent ounce of its power, and all that God is calling you to bring forth. We must honor the beckoning that we feel and hear within us. We must honor the divine purpose that flows through our very expression. Being deeply anchored with God, we have a solid and unshakable spiritual foundation. Your voice, anchored in the soul, resonates with impact far beyond even the words you speak. Your voice carries a sacred mission, purpose, and all the overflowing, glorious, and magnificent blessings therein.

Our voices transform reality, bring forth what has been hidden in silence, break boundaries, and transcend limitations. Your voice brings the fullness of our world into view as God moves through all of creation, every soul, life, and every woman. When I ponder all that God has laid before women, from the everyday responsibilities, the daunting trials to the promising vistas, the path is blazed by simple bravery: *to speak what is in your soul.* To speak with a bold, faithful knowing that the best will be, and it will be done.

In calling on God, you find God is calling on you. To honor the voice God has given you shapes consciousness, what is known, what is believed, what is possible, and what our world can be. Yet, to lift your voice is not a solitary act. It is a communion with God from the depths of your soul, faith, and trust and becomes a communion with the world around you. Together, recalling the words of Sojourner Truth, with many women, your voice becomes an overflowing blessing. The grace, boldness, and power of your voice rocks our world, restores, harmonizes, and enlightens it ... and turns our world right-side up again! Let your soul be bold and your voice be blessed and bring forth the mission God has entrusted in you.

Devotion

Dear God, I call out to You. Be my steady, powerful rock. Cover me endlessly with Your sovereign presence and grace. Fill me with Your power through all of my being—flowing through my soul, heart, and mind. Lord, let me be bold and strong, and may my faith be unwavering. Let me stand, live, and speak anchored in Your truth. May I always speak to Your glorious name and most magnificent vision. With my heart and soul, I honor all You have endowed in my life purpose. I pray for Your grace as I raise my voice to fulfill all You have called me to do. Amen.

Reflection

Boldness is a spiritual quality, as much a personal characteristic. Take a few minutes to reflect: What does it mean to you to be bold in your soul? When has this quality emerged within you?

Consider the meaning of strength as a spiritual quality. What does it mean to have strength in your own soul? What does it mean to you to be strengthened by God? Write specific instances or insights that come to mind.

Contemplate what is most important in your life now. How might spiritual strength and boldness support and empower you now? How might you call on God to deepen and expand this within you?

Write your own devotion here.

Feel the words within and share them boldly with God.

Group Discussion

Begin with your devotions and reflections on Day 26. Open with the question: What have you most boldly called upon God for? Why did this matter to you? Share what feels comfortable. Consider: Have you felt heard by God? How did this feel and impact you? Share specific examples. How can anchoring into your relationship with God strengthen you? To close: What do you feel compelled to boldly speak now? End with prayers, lifting the soul, and blessing the voice and calling of each woman.

Day 27

Let Your Voice Be Phenomenal

For it is God who is at work in you, both to will and to work for His good pleasure.

Philippians 2:13 NASB1995

She said it, and she meant it, "Unbought and Unbossed." Shirley Chisholm, a black woman, was unafraid, undeterred, and boldly running to be president, commander-in-chief of the United States. The spirit in her voice, the magnitude of the purpose she carried for uplifting people, shone through. In Shola Lynch's film, *Chisholm '72*, her presence seemed to be charged by a force deep within her. Long before the advance of women's rights and women's rising numbers in national leadership, she was a societal innovator. Her voice itself became a powerful stand that resonated with impact and expressed what belief, commitment, and a powerful voice can do. I was drawn, compelled to understand the source of her phenomenal voice.

While I, of course, would never speak to her directly, I leaned in to find a deeper spiritual meaning. It was not just her moving voice, nor her solid stand; it was a person, filled with so much power, as though she spoke with a great force. It was a force of unshakable strength and impact that created lasting influence as it rippled outward and touched others. I saw a force of unassailable faith so deeply rooted in the soul that its energy enlarged and overflowed without limit. I saw a woman's voice divinely, powerfully, and phenomenally connected with God.

Our history and world are full of phenomenal women who embrace their power and use their voices to do what compels them. Their voices radiate as though they embody a great power that moves within them, a faith that God is with them, that fills their presence. This phenomenon of fully embodied energy, a force of expression through women's voices, is not just found in famous leaders. The phenomenon is expressed in women who know God, absorb the full spiritual power of this sacred connection, and fully express through their lives and voices the depth of what God called them to do.

We know these women in our own lives, communities, workplaces, and even ourselves. Some captivate others with their legendary presence, love, and kindness. Some stand up for others, speak up in families and organizations, and dare to speak for what matters. Some are peace bringers, women who step forward without swords or armies, listen to their souls, and shudder not because of conflict or warring. With the sheer force of their being, they are women who fearlessly speak the truth, stretch the limits of society, and become a force for the greatest and highest good. Yet, the phenomenon of powerful voices is not only vocally expressed; it also flows from a deeply grounded sense of purpose.

The term "phenomenon" is often used to describe what is extraordinary. Yet, phenomena are not exceptional nor rare, nor lofty or beyond what is expected. The phenomenon is not out there, removed, and only to be witnessed and admired from afar. The phenomenon is found in the purposeful, wondrous unfolding of your own purpose, voice, and life. Your profoundly unique expression dwells within and beckons you to look inside of your own experience.

There, you honor the purpose in your own sacred being, and with the grandest vision imaginable, you behold the power, impact, and reach of your own voice.

This sublime honor and embodiment of your voice is an extraordinary, exceptional, and wondrous phenomenon. To embody is to make real, live, and express the depth of your calling that flows through your soul and all of your being. As a woman fully lifts her voice and expresses what God has entrusted in her, she radiates a profoundly brilliant light. Our voices become a powerful phenomenon that stirs souls and imaginations. A voice powered by God, reverberating with might, filled by the Spirit, infused with awesome essence of you, works for the highest good:

For it is God who is at work in you, both to will and to work for His good pleasure.
Philippians 2:13 NASB1995

Speaking with a voice that embodies the depth of your own soulful union with God serves a mighty, extraordinary purpose. To choose and decide to let your presence be filled with the Spirit of God, a force that inspires all, creates wonders. To say and proclaim—*God, work in me for Your highest good, as You will*—is a glorious phenomenon. The Scripture beckons me and draws my soul closer to God, as close as spiritually possible, wanting no distance or separation in my being from God, so that I am filled and overflowing. As I witness the phenomenon of women soulfully and courageously using their voices, I am drawn to the ultimate source, the light of God, and seek it in my own being. In the service of our grandest visions, we use our voices to speak boldly, beautifully, and phenomenally of all the Creator has purposed within our lives.

As I imagine the landscape of humanity, all that God has laid in this world, I see the profound power and possibility of women standing in our faith, embodying truth in our souls, and raising our voices for impact everywhere. Your voice manifests and amplifies your God-given work and makes it real through your powerful existence. To honor the phenomenal voice of your soul makes your grandest vision, what matters most in your life and calling, a reality.

Yet, it is a choice, a sacred one, to honor your voice and claim this phenomenal power as your own. Shirley Chisholm's words, "unbought and unbossed," have a spiritual meaning for me. To be "unbought" is for no one to "own you." You speak with unwavering certitude that your ultimate direction comes from the source in your soul. To be "unbossed" is to possess your own authority. With unshakable trust in your authority, you speak and act with the power of your vision. As you trust the voice God has given you, your voice expands and grows in the service of what you believe.

This belief, to speak on your vision, flows from commitment. Within the power of a phenomenal voice lies an embodied commitment to what matters most, buttressed by faith. The power of this voice overflows. It is truly a remarkable experience of the union of spirit, soul, and voice—a woman that cannot be vanquished, conquered, overcome, or denied. God creating and working through our very lives carries a divine impetus, as though you speak and stand with the force of the Almighty.

We have a sacred responsibility: to honor the voice of your soul and let your voice be phenomenal. We have a choice to shine or shrink. To dim your voice, turn it down, or to let your voice shine brilliantly. There is no limit to God working within us and no limit to a woman's voice attuned to the frequency of the Almighty God.

The impact and blessings are abundantly, radiantly, and gloriously overflowing.

The Scripture tells us it is God at work in us. This calls us to honor the Spirit. To feel and heed the urging in your soul, beckoning you to the great glory of God within your own life. This calls you to let your voice rise fully and place no limit on the God working through you. Embrace the awesomeness of the light within you—as light makes all things visible, our voices enlighten the fullness of God's plan and bring to the fore what must be told and heard.

You have a sacred decision—to step into your power and stand on the promises of God. Women honoring their souls, voices, and God write a new phenomenal story, not only for the few, brave, or historical but every woman who believes in the greatness God placed within her. At the heart of greatness lies devotion—to dedicate and pour all of oneself into your highest calling. When your soul becomes supremely aligned—indistinguishable from your purpose—powerful energy overflows.

In societal breakthroughs that advanced our world to a more loving place, brave souls connected to a force larger than themselves led the way. You may be blessed to have a supportive community, family, or a circle of women to cheer you on. Other times, your steps may be solitary. Yet, to raise your voice boldly, you are never alone. You are always standing in the light and in the power of the calling God has given you. Knowing you are standing with God, you honor the depth, meaning, significance, and purpose that your voice brings into the world.

Your voice magnifies and expands in unfathomable ways a part of God's incomprehensible plan. Give voice to all God has called you to do. Let it ripple outward, touch spirits and lives, and ignite the hearts and faith of many people. Trust what God beckons and let it fill you mightily. Let your voice be phenomenal.

Devotion

Dear God, let my voice be filled with Your power, energy, and grace. I place my soul, my purpose, and my works on Your altar. Let my voice expand with Your purposes. Attune me to Your beckoning, direction, and light. I pray to be filled with Your presence as I speak for the highest good. I thank you for my voice, for everywhere, and for everyone it is destined to touch. Surround me and ground me, dear Lord, with courage and clarity as I raise my voice to manifest great works in Your blessed creation. Thank you, God. Amen.

Reflection

Reflect for a moment on being phenomenal. Let this seep into your soul and imagine the "God's-eye" view of yourself. Consider: What do you most powerfully bring to life through your phenomenal voice? Write down all that arises.

Consider the meaning of God at work in you. What does that Scripture mean to you? How can this truth empower your voice?

Consider the authority of your own voice as a spiritual necessity. Take a few minutes and reflect: How can trusting your inner authority serve a higher purpose? When and where do you see this impact?

Write your own devotion here.

Stand and speak it aloud as a prayer to God.

Group Discussion

Open with your devotions and reflections on Day 27. Start with the question: What comes to mind when you think of a "phenomenal woman" and a "phenomenal voice?" Share examples. Do you consider your own voice phenomenal? Does "phenomenal" feel comfortable or true for you? Why or why not? Consider: What does it mean for God to lift your voice? How can honoring your phenomenal voice serve a greater purpose? Close with specific commitments to share your voice. End with prayers, lifting, and blessing the phenomenal voice of each woman.

THEME TEN

Behold Your Glorious Vision

To be a visionary can sound like an exalted ideal. To have a vision that moves and inspires others may seem to emanate from a blessed few who are endowed with extraordinary talent, guts, and drive. Yet, vision is not an extraordinary or rare gem but rather a power to be cultivated and unleashed. We find our vision within our own way of seeing all that is, all that can be, and all that will be done.

Lying beyond observation and what is perceived by the senses, vision emanates from the soul. Vision sees the brimming potential between your present moment and your blessed future. Vision honors the possibilities within you as a potent force of action. Vision bridges the gap between your current reality, with unwavering faith, that your boldest imagination will be done. Vision beholds each moment of life with profound gratitude as the precious seeds that manifest your cherished future.

In these next three days, we behold your glorious vision. Your way of seeing, rooted in your soul, propels powerful action. Your way of seeing, grounded in unshakeable faith, sees the most breathtaking visions and their ultimate fruition. Your way of seeing—all that you are, all that you behold, and all that God is—propels the most sacred, overflowing, and glorious vision of the woman God called you to be.

Day 28

To Manifest the Unbelievable

"Truly I tell you, if you say to this mountain, 'Be taken up and thrown into the sea,' and if you do not doubt in your heart, but believe that what you say will come to pass, it will be done for you."

Mark 11:23 NRSV

She witnessed the unthinkable. The tragic and unbelievable reality shook her to the core of being. For hours, she sat in her kitchen, still and unmoving. The scene replayed in her mind—walking home, gunfire erupted, a car was hit and careened out of control. It hit a woman and her three children. Sadly, they all lost their lives. Betty had lived through the violence and had relatives who died in the conflict in Northern Ireland. Yet, what she saw that day, propelled her to do something she had never done before.

She left her house and started knocking on doors. She told the women, we must do something—this violence must end. We must take a stand for peace. Her energy took over, spread, and awakened others. More and more women began knocking on doors, calling for peace. The local media caught wind of the story. Much to Betty's surprise, the women showed up amazingly, in massive droves, on the brilliant day of the rally.

From every direction, Protestant and Catholic women, whose sides were so bitterly divided and fighting in a war, converged on the scene. Together, the women stood for peace. They joined together with the belief that they could manifest the unbelievable—peace. The moment was seminal, a growing shift in the consciousness of the people. One year later, Betty Williams, along with Mairead Corrigan, won the Nobel Peace Prize in 1976 for their work for peace in Northern Ireland.

When I met Betty Williams and interviewed her decades later, her passion and vision were palpable. As she recounted the events of that day, she believed fervently that the tragedy she witnessed could no longer be. Betty committed herself, forcefully and passionately, to bring forth a new reality for the people of Northern Ireland. She took a bold stand, with determined vision, and spoke to the power of moving toward the unbelievable, with the mightiest of faith. The Scripture tells us this truth:

> *"Truly I tell you, if you say to this mountain, 'Be taken up and thrown into the sea,' and if you do not doubt in your heart, but believe that what you say will come to pass, it will be done for you."*
>
> *Mark 11:23* NRSV

This speaks to an unbelievably powerful vision. By having the unshakeable belief in your heart that the *incredible* can be done, it *will* be done. Yet, the force of this vision lies in love—fully possessed and all-encompassing. This love manifests the impossible. The very idea that a mountain could move conjures the unbelievable, transcending all rationality and evidence of what stands in front of you. The faith that moves a mountain is so connected and so compelled by love that there is no doubt, no inkling, thought, contemplation, or even consideration of failure. In faith, so utterly complete and certain, there remains *only* room for belief.

This belief closes the gap between reality and vision and flows from a greater working of God's power. A God-centered belief emboldens you to see beyond reality—that the present is a matter of circumstance, but that change is possible and can become reality. This belief endows your vision with power—that what you say *will* come to pass. Your vision becomes a spiritual force that engenders and inspires belief within you and overflows to others. With tenacity and commitment that never relinquishes the vision, the *unbelievable* becomes real.

Yet, to behold a vision of the unbelievable begins within. To be inwardly compelled to act on your vision begins inside a courageous heart. As I reflect on the story of Betty Williams, I most deeply resonate with how the movement started small—it began within her. Yet, it was not small in terms of expanse, possibility, or impact. The vision was only small in that it was personal—small enough to feel, know, and hold within your own soul as real. The vision is yours to act on, believe, and commit to, yet is upheld and expanded by the Almighty God.

With Betty, she had no intention, nor did she set out to be a leader of a national peace movement. She had her own family and had been working as a secretary. Yet, Betty felt a clear urging and vision in her heart and followed where it led. Her soul was determined, propelled her, and she moved. With unwavering faith and the undeniable vision of many women coming together as one, they manifested the unbelievable. Betty continued to devote her life to work for peace and founded an international organization to protect children. Truly, extraordinary visions and wondrous outcomes begin as a movement within the heart and soul.

While your vision can sometimes be amazingly clear, like an entire picture laid before you, it often requires a step into the unknown. Vision can flow as an urgent, loving compassion that compels you to act. Vision may flow from an undeniable conviction that pushes you to take a stand. It may begin in discord, birthed from a place of utter incongruence—that the present situation is no longer acceptable and must change. Yet, as the prospect of change can often bring fear and uncertainty, it is not always possible, probable, or necessary to rid yourself of all doubt. Instead, vision flows from a belief and faith, a forcefulness of the heart, that drives your decision to move forward.

In this way, as vision often begins as a sketch within, and not seeing the whole picture, we act on what we *desire* to manifest. We can never know completely what will happen when we act—the breadth of all that we will create and all those we will impact. Yet, with faith, your vision connects you to a much larger force. The faith that moves mountains is an indomitable faith in God that touches all and makes everything possible. With this faith, you tap into a far greater force within your being that ignites the power of your vision. To feel it within you, you behold the promise of your vision. Whether your vision gently whispers or strongly stirs you, with faith that moves mountains—it will come to pass.

As you scan the landscape of all that you imagine—every mountain already moved and the mountain that stands before you now—notice that the unimaginable expanse of God upholds the breadth of your vision. Notice the part within you that believes that the unbelievable can and will happen. Far beyond a mere idea, your vision is a reality, an occurrence unfolding in the very moment you are now in. The vision grows from within you and all you bring forward.

Vision is personal, sacred, and divine. Possibilities lie within your imagination and in your decision—what you determine to bring into existence. Betty Williams believed that a scene of violence could be a place of peace, despite seeing no evidence that this vision was possible. Yet, the women, collectively, had a conviction that they could do what had not yet been done. With the seed of belief sown into the steps of their historic stand for peace, they moved toward realizing their unbelievable vision. As a mighty tree grows from the tiniest seed, your grandest vision lies in the power of each small yet visionary step.

As you reflect on your vision, honor all that God has placed within your view. No matter how impossible or unbelievable, small or improbable, know it is meant to be. Your vision is a sacred path to trust and walk. It was divinely given to you—the woman God called you to be. Behold your glorious vision as God does, with all its overflowing grace, power, and potential. Behold your vision with unending faith and believe you can move mountains. And indeed, you shall.

Devotion

Dear God, I devote my heart courageously, boldly, and completely to You. Let me be filled with Your grandest, most astounding, and most glorious vision. May I be confident in what You have placed in my heart, mind, hand, and life to do. I pray that You show me the way amidst the impossible, unthinkable, and unbelievable. I pray that You fill my faith with a reservoir of Your grace and glory. I lift every vision I behold to You—may it manifest Your most magnificent power and purpose. In Jesus' name, I pray. Amen.

Reflection

Take a moment and consider exactly where you are now. Meditate on the questions: What stirs your heart now? What big idea or grand vision is beckoning you now to bring it forward?

Imagine the faith that can move a mountain. Think of an experience in your life where you tapped deeply into your faith. What did you learn and gain? What does it mean to you to have faith that moves mountains?

Consider the power of God that *moves* the mountains. Let this seep into your heart and let it expand your vision. How can your faith in God enable you to manifest your most extraordinary vision?

Write your own devotion here.

Hold it in your heart and vision. Speak it aloud as a prayer to God.

Group Discussion

Open with your devotions and reflections on Day 28. Start with the question: What does it mean to have a vision? Share a personal vision—a clear one or a vision now beginning to grow within you. Consider and share as comfortable: Do you trust your vision? Why or why not? What gives you confidence in your vision? For each woman: How can leaning into your faith expand and empower your vision? What does it mean to you for God to move the mountain? Close with prayers—lifting up the vision of each woman to God.

Day 29

To Imagine the Impossible

"Truly, truly I say to you, the one who believes in Me, the works that I do, he will do also; and greater works than these he will do; because I am going to the Father."

John 14:12 NASB2020

For years, these words of Jesus confounded me. I wondered: how could anyone do anything *greater* than all the miracles and works Jesus performed? The Scripture pushed me into my own contemplation, beyond the need to understand what the words meant through historical interpretations or even asking others for the true meaning. His words moved me to go within my own consciousness and challenged the very limits of my imagination.

The miracles of Jesus, God in the flesh amongst us, demonstrated the height and breadth of possibilities on earth. Yet, His words pushed me to consider—what if there is no limit or no ceiling? What if Jesus's works don't represent the depth and magnitude of what is possible? What if they reveal—simply and profoundly—all that is possible when we believe? And what if our calling is to do the greater works that are possible within us and in our lives, as we are called?

Jesus's words invite us into a powerful spiritual position. To believe so deeply in Jesus and all He has done, we know that greater works in overflowing numbers will be done through the lives of fervent, passionate, and committed believers. To know that my soul is attuned to the Almighty God, and all the possibilities therein, pushed me to imagine more than I ever thought possible. His words showed me the unquestioned boundaries on my own vision that had unknowingly and unconsciously limited what I even *conceived* as possible.

Quite unexpectedly, one sunny day, I ran headlong, painfully yet necessarily, into my own inner limit. It was hot, nearly 98 degrees, supposedly a mild day for Tempe, Arizona, in August. I decided to take a walk up the mountain. So ... it wasn't *really* a mountain; it was technically a butte, but still big! With my shoes laced and my water bottle filled, I was up for the challenge. I hadn't even walked more than 10 minutes up the mountain before I was hot! Hot, really hot, tired, and drained. I was so tired that I was panting, almost heaving, and felt every muscle in my diaphragm expand as though I was grasping for the next breath of air.

I looked to the top of the mountain, which seemed so far. I began rationalizing to myself. Even though my goal was to reach the summit, I already had gotten a much better workout than walking on the hotel treadmill. And the kicker, I probably burned triple the calories! I reasoned that I had accomplished much more today than I planned, and I most certainly earned the privilege of a very big and delicious dinner. I contemplated turning back. And then, I paused.

The moment was surreal—it was as if my own thoughts stood apart from me, and I could see my own thinking clearly. At that moment, I no longer wanted to own those thoughts: My rationalization, justification, and excuses for how far I should go were like an invisible line in my consciousness that rose up as a limit. That line, a previously untouched mental boundary, maintained an upper ceiling to my progress. Even though my inner dialogue was about a walk, it surfaced a way more significant realization. I had encountered an unconscious limitation, a smallness in my own thinking and imagination. I no longer felt comfortable holding a limit in my mind, my body, or any limit at all to the scope of my possibilities. Even though I was extra sweaty and hot, I decided—"I am going on."

As I continued walking, slowly with each step, I felt the inner boundaries dissolve. The part of me that assumed there was a limit, that the limit was even natural and normal, simply faded. As I reached the summit, I felt freedom ... a light expansiveness within me. I saw new vistas; even more mountains stretched out beyond. Although huge and in the distance, each mountain looked like a height I could now more easily scale—a mission I knew I could accomplish. My perception changed. The mountains became endless landscapes of possibilities for all I could achieve—far greater than I had ever imagined. I gained a more extraordinary view of beholding all that God has laid within me and before me to do.

Standing atop the mountain, I looked back to the place, halfway down, where I encountered my limit. There, I shed that restriction in my mind, body, and consciousness and walked right through it. Limits and boundaries become entrenched lines of what is already known, safe, believed, and done. Now, feeling triumphant, I beheld a powerful, new perspective. Looking at the mountains, I imagined what lies on the other side, pushing my imagination further than I ever conceived. I felt within—there is no limit to the works that can be done. It is all possible, as I embrace Jesus's words:

"Truly, truly I say to you, the one who believes in Me, the works that I do, he will do also; and greater works than these he will do; because I am going to the Father."

John 14:12 NASB2020

Jesus's words compel us to release every limit—conscious or unconscious, emotional or rational—on the possibilities within the broadest reaches of our calling and vision. I felt the need to push past any part of me and my own thinking that helped tether these limits to my life. Limits may be imposed by others and allowed by our own thoughts, but they are not God-given. With Christ, you have the glorious invitation to conceive and imagine all the works you can do when you believe.

Belief in the power of God enlarges and enriches our visions. When belief in God touches your soul, mind, and imagination, you move with certainty into the unknown. The seemingly impossible turns into a clear, steady path as you simply take the next step. We grow confident in the knowledge that what we behold in our visions will be done.

The greater works that you shall do are of paramount importance to the landscape of God's creation. When you break through your limits—in your thinking, vision, or even belief in God—you tap into a spiritual force that lifts your consciousness and holds all possibilities together. This force—overflowing, unbounded, and unlimited—flows through you and all the works that are yours to do. Yet, being upheld by the power of God, you are never working alone.

Our visions are greater, far greater than what we can achieve by sole personal effort. Faith in God stretches our imaginations and guides our visions. We see every impossibly grand goal, not only as real but overflowing with potential and promise. Our expansive belief bridges the spiritual gap between where we stand, what we see, and what lies beyond. With faith, we stand powerfully on the line of mystery between ourselves and God and shift to a new, higher center of gravity. With this blessed assurance, we leap into a faithful trust and move surely in the direction of all we behold.

The Scripture ultimately calls us to be as unbounded in our relationship with God as Jesus was. You are called to put no limits on all you can do in your sacred journey with God. Let your vision enlarge any boundaries within you and all that you conceive and envision in your life, purpose, and mission.

Even when you do not know how to begin, or if you feel unequipped or unprepared, when you see a vision that compels, stirs, and enlivens you, move toward it. Behold it as your vision, as the magnificence God has given you to bring forth on this blessed earth. Let the vistas of your imagination lead the way, and with your unending belief, the greater works within you will be done.

Devotion

Dear God, I lift my heart, soul, mind, and vision to You. I pray that You search me, fill me, inspire, guide, and lead me. I pray that You dissolve and break any boundaries within my mind and consciousness that limit or prevent Your most extraordinary works to be done in and through my life. I pray that You anoint my vision and all my steps with Your mighty grace. I thank you for Jesus and the blessed way He shows. May my faith, belief, and vision be blessed and filled with Your light. In Jesus's name, I pray. Amen.

Reflection

Take a pause and meditate for 10 minutes on the Scripture. Hold the words in your mind and heart. What "greater work" is possible, speaking to you and calling you now? Write down all that comes up.

Touch your heart and consider your own belief. Feel how it moves through you. Notice any places of disconnect or limitation, openness or strength. How can you more deeply cultivate belief in your own possibilities and belief in God? Write down all that you hear.

Imagine if you had absolutely no boundaries on yourself, in your mind, or what you thought possible for a goal, dream, or vision. How would this unlimited state empower you? What vision would you pursue?

Write your own devotion here.

Hold it in your heart and mind. Speak it aloud as a vision to God.

Group Discussion

Begin with your devotions and reflections on Day 29. Consider: What does it mean to be unbounded and unlimited in your vision? Share examples and ideas. Have you had that experience, and what did it mean to you? Conversely, have you felt limited or restricted in your vision? How did that feel, and what was the impact? For each woman: How can belief in God expand your vision and propel you to move toward it? Close with a statement of your most powerful vision now. End with prayer—lifting up each woman's vision to be gloriously blessed by God.

Day 30

To Be Grateful for All that Is

"I glorified you on earth by finishing the work that you gave me to do."

John 17:4 NRSV

In moments of pause, unwinding after a rough day or a glorious one, I often say, *"Thank you, dear Lord. Thank you. Thank you for all that is, for all that is within me, and all that is mine to do on this earth."* Gratitude is a powerful prayer. We find joy and meaning in the moments of life, from the mundane to the miraculous. Gratitude plumbs the depths of even the most painful or tragic life occurrences and reaches the part of your soul that flows always and seeks life still. Filled with gratitude, we explore the depths of everything, all that we accomplish and all that leads us to the next glorious vista. Gratitude becomes a powerful vision, a way of seeing, to behold not only the past but to deeply appreciate your life now.

With gratitude, we appreciate the binding force of God, the glorious traces of grace, purpose, and love that holds all of life together. Life unfolds in the blessed connectedness of each moment. Everything that has occurred has led to the present. All that will occur rests in the moment now. And every step matters.

Gratitude engenders appreciation and awareness of each moment, day, week, and phase of life. Your vision expands your lens and allows you to see the purpose and power in every step you have taken. God has been lighting your path—every single step. With gratitude, you behold your own existence even more deeply, profoundly, and beautifully.

Gratitude makes the simple sublime. In the summer evenings, I am grateful to live near a river, and I often walk by the water at sunset. I treasure the change in the sky as the evening approaches, as streaks of warm, golden blush hues slowly leave their impressions on the horizon. I am grateful for this view and the people enjoying it all—the families, the walkers, bikers, elderly couples sitting on benches, ducks gliding by, and baby birds chirping. As a light wind rustles the trees and stirs the waters, it is as though an omniscient force lightly touches everything and everyone.

In those still moments, I am grateful for the very precious moment of life now. I am thankful for the past, what is over, completed, accomplished, and done. I ponder all that lies ahead in moments yet to unfold. Yet, there is now. I cherish the sacred, incredible present and am grateful for it all.

Our gratitude becomes a lived prayer. The message unfolds throughout your life, as though the very expression of your life is a gift, a powerful offering. I am aware and grateful for this breath, this life, and this beating heart that prays, talks, and calls on God. I am grateful, attuned to the sacred moment now, as the incomprehensible breath of God touches and enlivens me, you, and all of life.

We can behold life as a sacred gift, as we bring forth our purposes, loves, missions, joys, and visions into existence. The moments, our mornings, days, evenings, and years are the substance of the gift of life. Gratitude lets us behold our own lives with awe and reverence. To see the magnitude of it all, we can be grateful to God for the works, purpose, and calling that is ours. As life unfolds, we have a grateful vision for all that God has given us to do. The words of Jesus give us a sacred prayer:

"I glorified you on earth by finishing the work that you gave me to do."
John 17:4 NRSV

This vision, this way of seeing with gratitude, lets me appreciate the lifelong journey we are on with God. Our journeys are not simply a series of lessons or accomplishments or work. Rather, we *are* the magnificent work, a sacred masterpiece, unfolding and living. Your life is the work that God has given you. Whether routine, extraordinary, cherished, or complex, your life and all the purposes therein is the work you have been called to do.

Our work unfolds through all of life. Our purposes grow through careers, expands through mothering, loving neighbors and husbands, and taking care of grandmas and aunties as they age. Our work extends through our conversations with friends, strangers, and the talks we have with God. Through it all, with gratitude, we glimpse the overflowing grace that moves, that is God, and dwells in our lives.

Every juncture of life—whether a mistake or an inspired lesson, an ending, or a loving reconciliation—is the substance of your work. Whether you stumble, break down or reach the highest height, it is your journey and work to do. Gratitude connects your heart, soul, life, and every experience with God. To be filled with overflowing, joyous gratitude, pray and declare—*thank you, God, for the woman you have called me to be.*

In the mornings, my prayer practice is a time to simply sit, have coffee, savor the quiet, and talk to God. There, I am still—grateful and attuned to recognizing and allowing whatever flows. I share my thoughts and open my heart to hear, be filled, and receive. This morning prayer time is not grand nor elaborate. Rather, it is what I need—what my soul needs. Simply, I need this time to feel present and grounded in gratitude for my connection with God. So much flows from those moments. Flashes of insight, clarity, and breakthroughs often occur. Other times, on many days, the feeling of being connected, peaceful, and grateful simply deepens and grows.

Gratitude lets us say *thank you* for our own lives. You have been given a sacred gift to fully open and live—your life and your wondrous calling. The grace of the Almighty flows through the gift, all you are, your every step, and all that God has entrusted in your existence to overflow from your life.

As much as we plan, set our steps, or surrender, we can be grateful for the divine trajectory of our life journey. Our vision is sharpened when we dwell in gratitude and let it be the heartbeat that drives our mindset, imagination, and approach to our life calling. We will encounter challenges, setbacks, opportunities, mountains and valleys, and many moments that will confound and amaze us. For all of it, be grateful. To behold all that has been, to see God's grace along the way, we have a vision of what ultimately matters most.

This work that glorifies God rests in you. Treasure the thought of using your life and your soul to glorify God. What an awesome blessing to receive the light of God flowing through your soul—every work, love, relationship, and mission God has given you. To behold life with the end in mind, for your life and works to be gloriously done and lived, you become a sacred and overflowing vessel of God's grace on this earth.

We find, feel, and express the glory of God throughout our days. We behold each moment and all that lies before us with gratitude. To profoundly appreciate how God beholds you, you see the glory of your own blessed walk as the woman God called you to be. Our gratitude is a powerful choice, way, and vision. Yet, gratitude becomes a much larger force that encircles us all.

This larger force reminds me of a communion circle. After someone is baptized, the church members gather in a large circle, each person holding hands, a blessed tie, with the newest person who devoted her life to Christ. In this circle, we hold a vision of love, faith, and gratitude and more beautifully hold each other. We are grateful for the love of Christ now consciously, purposely expressed through this life. A life that says I am grateful, surrendered to the magnificent God that moves, touches, and holds me. A life that says I see His glory, feel it, will live it, and it is *well* with my soul.

For the journey, for the calling God has given you, for every moment you have walked with God, whether uncertain or steady, let your soul be filled with gratitude. Let your soul see clearly, you *are* the work, and you *will* do all that God has *called* you to do. You can live with a depth of knowing that in every single blessed step you walk with God, you glorify and finish that work God has given you to do.

Devotion

Dear Lord, I am eternally grateful for Your love, presence, and grace that overflows all the days of my life. I am grateful for our blessed and sacred connection as I live my purpose, calling, and life journey. May Your love always overflow, pouring in and through me. May I behold my life and the work You have given me with abiding gratitude. Thank you for all You have entrusted in me and the woman You called me to be. In all my life, I will glorify You and finish the work You have given me to do.

Reflection

Take a few moments to reflect on gratitude. Hold the energy and feeling within. What are you most grateful for now—in your life and in who you are? How does gratitude shape your perspective on how you see your life?

Think for a moment about an experience that was hard or challenging. How can viewing that experience through a lens of gratitude shape your perspective? What do you gain, understand, and appreciate now about the experience?

Reflect for a moment on the Scripture for Day 30. Imagine the God's-eye view of your heart, soul, and life, and God's presence through all of your life, connecting everything. How does gratitude guide your vision and calling? Freely write all that comes up.

Write Your Own Devotion Here.

Hold it in your heart with gratitude and speak it aloud to God as a prayer.

Group Discussion

Begin with your devotions and reflections on Day 30. Take a moment to go within and reflect on yourself with gratitude. What are you most grateful for—in the woman God called you to be? What qualities, desires, and ways of being are you most grateful for? Consider your life and all you do. What do you see differently when you view your life with gratitude? Finally, for all: What are you most grateful for in the journey you have shared with each other? Close with a prayer circle—lifting each woman up, her calling, and your journey together with gratitude to God.

Conclusion

Imagine, if you will, a life supremely lived. As you near its ultimate fulfillment, you may now behold what lies beyond. I can only imagine crossing an unfathomable threshold and coming face to face with God. Here, we may finally grasp the summation of life, all that had been sought and desired, prayed for and worked for, contemplated, rationalized, and finally surrendered. I pray that our souls will be at peace with God, filled with the truth that we lived and answered our call.

I hope that every ounce of what God placed in your soul shines eternally brightly. I pray that our lives are well-lived, well-loved, and the calling, the glorious journey is complete. And, while we do not know the length of our lives, the certainty of its conclusion endows life with great purpose and meaning.

As you live your calling, I pray that the entire depth of your sacred relationship with God is explored—that no emotion, no thought, no dream, no desire, no care, no love is left untouched. I pray that all the Creator has given you will be gloriously manifest through, and in, and because of your life. It is a mighty call to answer your calling—to rise, stand, and live as the woman God called you to be. I pray that you behold fully all that has been, all that can be, and will be in your wondrous life. I pray that all the love, grace, and blessing that God can bestow on you is, indeed, sacred and overflowing.

References

Britt Chole, Alicia. 2006. Anonymous: Jesus' hidden years...and yours. Nashville: Thomas Nelson.

Britt Chole, Alicia. 2018. *Anonymous: TBN Original Series.* Fort Worth, TX: Trinity Broadcasting Network.

Dunson, Konyka. 2007. *In Depth with Konyka Dunson: A Conversation with Betty Williams.*

Ensler, Eve. 1996. *The Vagina Monologues.*

Hooks, Bell. 2000. All about love: new visions. New York: William Morrow and Company, Inc.

Lessac, Michael. 2007. *Truth in Translation.*

Lynch, Shola. 2005. *CHISHOLM '72: Unbought & Unbossed.*

Shange, Ntozake. 1989. For Colored Girls Who Have Considered Suicide When the Rainbow Is Enuf: A Choreopoem. New York: Collier Books.

Spielberg, Steven. 1985. *The Color Purple.* United States: Warner Bros.

Truth, Sojourner. 1851. *Ain't I a Woman?* Akron, Ohio. Women's Rights Convention. *(As recounted by Frances Gage, in 1863)*

Truth, Sojourner and Gilbert, Olive. 1997. Narrative of Sojourner Truth. Mineola, NY: Dover Publications.

Vanzant, Iyanla. 1997. The Value in the Valley: A Black Woman's Guide through Life's Dilemmas. New York: Fireside.

Williamson, Marianne. 1996. A Return to Love: Reflections on the Principles of a Course in Miracles. New York: HarperCollins.

About the Author

Konyka Dunson is an author, inspirational speaker, and transformational workshop leader who speaks with a mission—for women to unleash the power of their souls and all they were born to do. Her passion for catalyzing deep-rooted impact began as a public high school mathematics teacher, where she relished gathering her students for conversation circles to discuss their views and ideas. Konyka went on to have a 20-year career in education spanning the leadership of educational program initiatives, conference planning, and higher education administration.

Yet, a radio volunteer opportunity unleashed her creative soul. At WPFW 89.3 FM, Konyka co-hosted the women's collective, "Sophies Parlor," and hosted her own weekly show, "The Sol Rise Experience," a blend of uplifting interviews, jazz, and world music. She excelled as a top radio station fundraiser and created her own television talk show, "In Depth with Konyka Dunson," that won the Alliance for Community Media Award for Best Entertainment Talk Show. Konyka highlighted women's voices in health issues, ending violence, national leadership, and forging peace. She later produced "MOST TV" for Men Can Stop Rape, giving young men a voice on violence prevention. Konyka produced and hosted several Washington, DC premieres of documentary films bringing the arts, social issues, and powerful conversations to widespread audiences.

Driven to create breakthrough conversations, Konyka speaks, coaches, trains, and facilitates workshops to equip mission-driven leaders to achieve positive change. As a Gallup-Certified Strengths Coach, Take Flight with DISC Trainer and Personify Leadership Trainer, Konyka is an expert in leveraging industry assessments to help organizations realize their greatest possibilities. She holds a BA in Economics from Wake Forest University, MA in Social Foundations of Education from the University of Maryland at College Park, and is a proud graduate of Docs in Progress, where she co-produced her first documentary short, "A Story of Service." She is now pursuing doctoral studies in leadership and public dialogue at the University of the District of Columbia.

Konyka, who grew up in the church and was always a spiritual seeker, had a poignant, deeply reflective, and conscious walk to God. Baptized at 38, she served on missions in Kenya and Haiti, where she became convicted that faith must lie at the heart and foundation of her work. As a co-author in *Messages to My Younger Self: Messages to Nourish and Heal the Soul,* she encourages women to honor the voice of their soul and centers her mission—her speaking, coaching, and every engagement—in this sacred call. Konyka passionately believes—our world most needs and is blessed and uplifted by the visions in the souls of women.

Continue Your Journey

To invite Konyka to speak at your next event and for inquiries on book circles, workshops, and coaching, please contact:

info@KonykaDunson.com
www.KonykaDunson.com

Stay connected and continue the conversation:

@KonykaTV

CPSIA information can be obtained
at www.ICGtesting.com
Printed in the USA
LVHW050821190122
708682LV00011B/361

9 781737 558231